ORGANIZING CHANGE

ORGANIZING CHANGE

An Inclusive, Systemic Approach
to Maintain Productivity and Achieve Results

William W. Lee • Karl J. Krayer

Pfeiffer
A Wiley Imprint
www.pfeiffer.com

Published by Pfeiffer
An Imprint of John Wiley & Sons, Inc.
989 Market Street, San Francisco, CA 94103-1741   www.pfeiffer.com

For additional copies/bulk purchases of this book in the U.S. please contact (800) 274-4434.

Pfeiffer books and products are available through most bookstores. To contact Pfeiffer directly call our Customer Care Department within the U.S. at (800) 274-4434, outside the U.S. at (317) 572-3985 or fax (317) 572-4002.

Pfeiffer also publishes its books in a variety of electronic formats. Some content that appears in print may not be available in electronic books.

ISBN: 0-7879-6443-3

Library of Congress Cataloging-in-Publication Data
Lee, William W.
   Organizing change : an inclusive, systemic approach to maintain
productivity and achieve results / by William W. Lee and Karl J. Krayer.
      p. cm.
Includes bibliographical references and index.
   ISBN 0-7879-6443-3 (alk. paper)
   1. Organizational change—Management. I. Krayer, Karl J., 1954- II. Title.
   HD58.8.L423 2003
   658.4′06—dc21   2002155390

Acquiring Editor: *Matthew Davis*
Director of Development: *Kathleen Dolan Davies*
Developmental Editor: *Susan Rachmeler*
Editor: *Rebecca Taff*
Senior Production Editor: *Dawn Kilgore*
Manufacturing Supervisor: *Becky Carreño*
Cover Design:
Printing   10   9   8   7   6   5   4   3   2   1

To my dad, Walter W. Lee.
BILL

To my wife, Kim, and our beautiful children, Emily Joyce
and Kristen Belle, and to the memory of my mother,
Joyce Louise Lundberg, who still inspires me today.
To all of my friends in my professional and
fraternal organizations who have expressed
confidence in me.
KARL

CONTENTS

List of Figures, Exhibits, and Tables xi

Preface xiii

Introduction 1

UNIT ONE: REQUIREMENTS FOR CHANGE

1. **Change and the Growth and Complexity of Organizations 15**

   Overview 15

   Organizing Change 18

2. **Introduction to the Model 21**

   Overview 21

   Purpose of the Model 22

   Overview of the Model 22

   Advantages of the Model 26

vii

UNIT TWO: STAKEHOLDERS

3. Change Agents 29

Overview 29

Duties of Stakeholders 30

4. Choosing Committee Members 39

Overview 39

The Nature of Committees 40

Options for Selecting Members 40

5. Analyzing and Improving Committee Interaction 45

Overview 45

Interaction Styles 46

Rating and Analyzing Interaction 49

UNIT THREE: PROCESS

6. Planning 59

Overview 59

Inputs 60

Outputs 60

Responsibilities/Activities 60

Assigning Roles and Responsibilities 66

Case Study 71

7. Assessment 89

Overview 89

Inputs 89

Outputs 90

Responsibilities/Activities 90

Methodology for Conducting an Assessment 95

Case Study 96

8. Analysis 107

Overview 107

Inputs 107

Outputs 108

Responsibilities/Activities 108

Methodology for Conducting an Analysis 111

Case Study 124

9. Design 137

Overview 137

Inputs 137

Outputs 137

Responsibilities/Activities 138

Procedure for Conducting an Instructional Analysis 141

Procedure for Completing a Project Assessment 141

Procedure for Writing Objectives 145

Case Study 148

10. Development 159

Overview 159

Inputs 159

Outputs 159

Responsibilities/Activities 160

Case Study 164

11. Implementation 171

Overview 171

Inputs 171

Outputs 172

Responsibilities/Activities 172

Case Study 175

12. Evaluation 181

   Overview 181

   Inputs 181

   Outputs 182

   Responsibilities/Activities 182

   Data Analysis 186

   Return on Investment 187

   Constructing Instruments 190

   Evaluation Plan and Report 192

   Case Study 195

UNIT FOUR: COMMUNICATION

13. Gathering Information 203

   Overview 203

   Quality and Quantity of Information During Change 203

   Communication in a Change Context 204

   Fact-Finding 205

   Communication Tactics to Gather Information 210

   Methods for Gathering Information 217

14. Disseminating Information 225

   Overview 225

   Kickoff 226

   Routine Dissemination 228

   Conducting Meetings 229

   Releases and Memos 234

Conclusion 235

References 241

About the Authors 245

Index 249

How to Use the CD-ROM 255

LIST OF FIGURES, EXHIBITS, AND TABLES

Figure P.1   The Continuum of Training, Human Performance,
              and Organizational Effectiveness xiv
Figure 2.1   The "Cube" 23
Exhibit 4.1   Innovation Checklist 42
Exhibit 4.2   Scoring Form 43
Table 5.1   Interaction Roles in Groups 47
Exhibit 5.1   Practice for Analyzing Interaction Roles 51
Table 6.1   Responsibilities During Planning 61
Exhibit 6.1   Project Management Tool 69
Exhibit 6.2   Sample Completed Project Management Tool 70
Table 7.1   Responsibilities During Assessment 91
Table 8.1   Responsibilities During Analysis 109
Exhibit 8.1   Skill Gap Analysis Tool 113

Exhibit 8.2   Extant Data Analysis Form 116

Exhibit 8.3   Issue Analysis Form 119

Exhibit 8.4   Issue Rating Form 122

Exhibit 8.5   Technology Analysis Tool 123

Table 9.1   Responsibilities During Design 138

Exhibit 9.1   Instructional Analysis Tool 142

Exhibit 9.2   Project Assessment Tool 143

Exhibit 9.3   Objectives Worksheet 146

Table 10.1   Responsibilities During Development 160

Exhibit 10.1   Project Plan 161

Table 11.1   Responsibilities During Implementation 172

Table 12.1   Responsibilities During Evaluation 182

Figure 12.1   Productivity Curve 184

Exhibit 12.1   Cost Calculation Template 189

Exhibit 12.2   Evaluation Plan and Report 193

Figure 13.1   Levels of Communication in Change 205

Exhibit 14.1   Sample Agenda for Change Steering Committee 232

Exhibit 14.2   Sample Narrative Agenda 233

PREFACE

WHAT IS YOUR DEPARTMENT OR DIVISION'S perceived value to your organization? Is your department likely to be one of the first impacted by downsizing when the organization is required to save money? We have seen this happen all too often in today's corporate environment, which is filled with peaks and valleys of profit and loss. Our analysis is that departments and divisions that are impacted the most during restructuring and reorganization are those that are disconnected from the goals of the organization and that failed to operate as an added value during tough economic downturns.

This book will move your department, division, and organization where it needs to be, given the state of the corporate environment today—to a position of value, operating with organizational savvy, where you both anticipate and solve problems that are important to its vision, mission, and objectives. This transformation can only occur when you are prepared to organize a change initiative designed to further not just yourselves, but also the organization.

Let's look at an example in a context that we have worked in collectively for almost forty years: Training. As we write this book, three distinct groups exist in the organization that touch this function: Training, human performance improvement, and organizational effectiveness. We perceive the skills inherent in these three groups to be quite compatible and on a continuum of low to high perceived value to the organization, as demonstrated in Figure P.1.

How, then, can a traditional training department increase value? The answer lies in the transformation from a department that "teaches skills" to one that "improves processes" that are important to the bottom line of the organization. Today's training group can move to the human performance level, and on to an organizational effectiveness level. How do you do that? By following a model that we have taken from traditional instructional design and using it to encompass a greater scope of issues.

We think that any department or division in an organization can make a similar transformation by organizing a change initiative with our model. We include a stakeholder component that explains how you can organize change to include all the impacted or affected parts of an organization. We include a process that describes the roles and responsibilities that key players

Figure P.1. The Continuum of Training, Human Performance, and Organizational Effectiveness.

Perception of value through connecting to the overall organization

Low   High

Training	**Human Performance**	**Organizational Effectiveness**
• Learning • Education • Skills	• Transfer of learning, education, and skills to the workplace • Workforce improvement	• Finding the scope of organizational issues • Process improvement

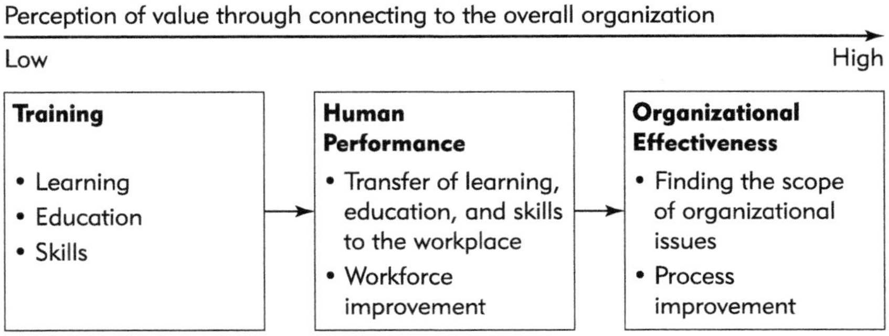

enact during seven phases of change. We end by discussing communication, which we think is highly necessary to keep all the stakeholders informed of what is happening and as a gauge to determine the kind of buy-in the initiative receives.

We are excited to have you with us as we travel through the three components of our model to organize change.

INTRODUCTION

WE HAVE ALL HEARD the popular line "the only constant is change." You can agree with that statement and then choose to take one of several very different directions. You can lead change, manage change, resist change, cope with change, or even "change" change.

This book is about organizing change. Our purpose in writing this book is to allow you to "get it right the first time." When you are finished with this book, you will understand how to involve the right people and have them perform the right tasks that will produce a successful change initiative for your organization.

Our assumption is that change initiatives are successful when they have breadth and depth in an organization, meaning that large numbers of affected employees are involved and represented. We call this approach "inclusive" and "systemic." We also assume that the more organized a change initiative is, the more the organization can maintain productivity and results as it transforms itself during the initiative. We do not believe that an organization must suffer as it undertakes a change initiative by operating in a chaotic manner resulting in unanticipated turnover, lost market share, lower sales, and decreased profits. An organized change initiative allows for stability in productivity and results.

Who Should Use This Book?

If you are an organizational development consultant, Human Resources professional, or organizational change agent, you have experience with and knowledge of various change models. You can benefit from this book as a working tool that you can use on a regular basis, with tools and ideas to supplement the materials you already have. The book and CD-ROM include a variety of checklists, worksheets, templates, and forms that you can use to assist you in organizing change initiatives.

As a line or staff manager in any type of department and in any organization, you can use the book to make and organize change initiatives within your own work group. You probably do not have formal training in change management, so you will want to use this book as a manual to lead you phase-by-phase through the change you are initiating, so that you can get it right the first time. Without a process to follow, you can make mistakes that will lose credibility for yourself and your proposed change initiative, as well as waste time and money. This book can help you avoid the pitfalls that people normally experience when the effort is haphazard. In addition, while you are making the change within your group, you are developing a valuable skill that will enhance you professionally in the future. With a successful operational change, your efforts will be recognized through the results you obtain.

University professors can also adopt the book as a text to teach our model to students in the fields of organizational behavior, organizational development, Human Resources, human performance technology, and instructional technology. It is not enough any longer for groups to study only their own discipline; they must know about other related disciplines as well. Change management is an associated field in all five of the disciplines listed above. Because the model we feature in this book is systematic and broken into manageable milestones, students can learn the mechanics of managing change that they must master before they can internalize the model.

A system of tools is provided on the CD-ROM that accompanies this book. These tools all work together to capture all relevant information and tie together each aspect of the initiative.

Why We Wrote This Book

Our belief in the positive aspects of change led us to write this book. Bill Lee worked for a large manufacturing organization in 1995 that decided it needed to change its production and distribution processes to make them more effective and efficient. Bill was assigned to the project to capture any information that might require training on the changes in the process. The project manager was a very bright and energetic engineer. However, he had no project management skills. The first meeting was a near disaster! Chaos reigned and the manufacturing and distribution divisions immediately began to lobby each other to change their process.

Bill watched as the fear of doom began to settle over the project manager's face. Being more detached from the interdepartmental "jockeying," Bill began to think of how he could help the manager gain control of the group and achieve a successful result. But Bill didn't know anything about project management either! What did he know? The instructional design process. So he began to think of how what he knew could be applied to a much broader issue than just designing training. Suddenly it dawned on him that the process was a near-perfect fit.

Bill waited until after everyone left the meeting and then approached the project manager and asked whether he could help in any way to organize the project. Bill briefly outlined the instructional design process on a whiteboard, explaining what each phase was for and what resulted from it. The project manager caught it right away—remember, we said he was a smart guy. So they set about laying out the project. At the next meeting, the project manager outlined the project plan for the entire group. They all bought in to the plan, which also got them away from coming to the meeting with a conclusion in mind, and instead set them to investigating.

They needed tools to capture data and then organize it. Bill would make drafts the morning before the meeting and send them to the project manager. He would make a few revisions, send them back, and Bill would bring the final versions to the meetings. The team sometimes discovered they needed a tool or worksheet in the middle of a meeting, so they would all work together to draft one then and there. So that took care of the process.

But who was going to be responsible for what? Maybe they needed to assign roles and responsibilities. At first either everyone wanted responsibility so they would have control or, if the responsibility was too great, they wanted to offload it onto the project manager. To solve the issue, we added not only responsibilities but, if someone had a responsibility that impacted another person, then the other person had to be consulted about a decision before it was finalized. If someone had neither responsibility nor was impacted by a decision, he or she was told about it at the end through some sort of "communication" either at a project meeting or through e-mail.

Ah, yes, "communication!" How would they get information out to everyone so there was a consistent message? They found out the need for communication the hard way when they began to find that everyone they talked to had received a different message. Employees from the manufacturing or distribution departments would stop the project manager and ask: "What's this I hear about [some subject or topic discussed at the meeting]?" Often the information the employee had was totally inaccurate. The project manager asked for and obtained an administrative assistant assigned to the project. She would take notes during the meeting and publish them within an hour after the meeting was over. The project team also decided at the end of every meeting what information needed to be e-mailed to everyone in the company.

Thus was born the three aspects of the model: The process, the stakeholders, and communication. After the project, Bill refined the tools and organized them so they could be used again, which they have been for other initiatives in other organizations.

Bill had known Karl Krayer for a long time through their membership in the American Society for Training and Development (ASTD) and knew he had a lot of experience with organizations that had gone through change.

Bill also knew he was a writer. So Bill asked Karl to join the project to give it a broader perspective.

Karl's perspective on organizational change was first-hand, in academic, corporate, and non-profit contexts. As a training manager for Dr Pepper/ Seven-Up, Inc., he assisted the vice president of the marketing services division in undertaking significant changes in operations for each of its five constituent departments. He has led strategic change initiatives for merged companies, fraternal organizations, academic departments, and churches. In addition, he has dodged, as well as been the victim of, a layoff. Karl and Bill have presented the model you will read about in this book at numerous professional conferences and association meetings.

In Defense of Change

Many people claim that they do not like change in most facets of their lives, especially on their jobs. We disagree. We think that what people dislike is the doubt and uncertainty that often accompany change. They do not like chaotic change. They do not like change that is unsystematic. They do not like change that "the select few" plan and impose on "the many." When only a few people plan and execute a change initiative in secrecy, speculation and rumors run rampant, negativity takes root, and, by the time the organization is ready to implement the change, resistance has already been strongly implanted in the minds of those who will be affected.

We believe that if an organization keeps people involved, informed, and represented during a change initiative, people are less likely to resist the effort. The reality is that, in most organizations, senior management initiates change. Whenever change is imposed exclusively from the top, many of those below will resist because employees simply perceive the initiative as an effort by management to impose its will. Conversely, when an idea for change comes from the line or staff employees, management's attitude is usually "What do they know?"

Some resistance always accompanies change. There will be those who champion the change and get on board immediately, some who wait to see what happens, and some who resist. The largest group is actually the "wait and see's." While the model we detail in this book can assist representatives of all three groups, those who belong to the "wait and see" cadre can easily be brought on board by the methods we discuss here.

Most authors of books take a passive and reactive approach to change. Their perspective is that "change is inevitable"; thus, they cover topics such as how to manage, survive, and adapt under conditions of change. Implicitly, their books seem to embrace the idea that the organization would rather not undergo change (Burns, 1993; Jeffreys, 1995; Noer, 1995; Pritchett & Pound, 1992, 1993). In this book, we take a different approach, which is proactive and positive. We begin with the idea that an organization deems that change is desirable and then must determine how to best accomplish it.

Other books take a systematic approach, but stop short by failing to specify the roles and responsibilities of the individuals who must turn the steps into action. For example, Kotter's works, *Leading Change* (1996) and *The Heart of Change* (2002), describe eight steps for managing change, but do not explain what agents or anyone steering the change specifically must do to enact the steps. Our book not only describes seven phases in the process, but also specifies the exact roles and responsibilities that various stakeholders enact.

Authors such as Gary Hamel (2000) in *Leading the Revolution* and Michael Useem (2001) in *Leading Up* make clear the point that the opportunity to initiate and lead change is not restricted to those at the top of an organizational hierarchy. We agree with this premise and, therefore, take an inclusive approach to change that involves widespread participation throughout the organization.

Our observation after participating in numerous change initiatives over the years is that most are not very well organized or thought out. Often, the impact of a change initiative that focuses on one part or process of an organization adversely affects other parts or processes of the organization. Due to a failure to organize a change initiative in a systemic way, champions of change typically fail to consider or misjudge these interaction effects.

For example, downsizing has typically been the first change initiative organizations consider during an economic downturn because it is a "quick" way to cut spending. However, of all of the companies that have downsized in order to improve performance, only 25 percent have achieved the results they desired (McGarvey, 2002). This occurs because companies fail to take into consideration the amount of work that remains, which must now be performed by fewer employees. Those employees who remain soon burn out and begin to search for more satisfying jobs elsewhere. When these companies decide to rebuild, they must hire new employees to perform the tasks, many of whom will be on new learning curves as they acclimate to the culture. Thus the company pays several times over—for the initial loss of productivity due to fewer workers, for additional lost productivity due to departures and training time, and for the loss of expertise that departing employees take with them.

Levels of Change

We think that it is important to define meaningful change and to differentiate it from other efforts that also carry the change label. In order to do this, we refer to Smith (1997), who identifies seven non-progressive levels of change:

1. *Effectiveness*—Doing the right things
2. *Efficiency*—Doing the right things right
3. *Improving*—Doing things better
4. *Cutting*—Doing away with thing
5. *Copying*—Doing things others are doing
6. *Different*—Doing things no one else is doing
7. *Impossible*—Doing things that can't be done

While all levels are beneficial, Smith states that 1 and 2 represent normal thinking, 3 represents continuous improvement, 4 and 5 represent interesting thinking, and 6 and 7 represent where real and meaningful change occurs.

What this says is that when you are going to initiate a change in your organization, do not aim for effectiveness and efficiency (such as downsizing), nor settle for minor adjustments, nor implement only what other organizations are doing. Real change occurs when people think differently and believe in the impossible. It takes courage to make real change.

The model we describe in this book targets these last two levels. Here are a few reasons we say this. First, we take an active approach to change. We use a model and describe a process with which you organize rather than simply react to change. You can only do things differently or tackle the impossible if you are driving the initiative forward. Second, the process we describe links to a vision of where the organization wants to be in the future. By definition, the vision is a desired state that should be a "stretch" to achieve, and our process contains an assessment of the gap between where the organization is and where the organization wants to go. The vision serves as an anchor for all of the components, activities, and principles. Third, because the process is inclusive, an organization can make full use of the talents, viewpoints, and contributions from all levels in its hierarchy. Often the people who *do* the work, rather than oversee the work, have the most innovative and forward-thinking ideas for how to change or overhaul a process and, therefore, implement real change. Fourth, the process contains numerous checks and balances, thus assuring that what may seem impossible or implausible actually becomes reality.

In the two case studies that you will read, the focal organizations undertake some remarkable new ways of doing work that entail risk. They also initiate their changes "their own way," rather than using a copycat or "cookie-cutter" approach adapted from another organization. We hope these case studies inspire you to aim for Levels 6 and 7 as you initiate a change for your organization.

Our goal is for you to implement change initiatives that reflect the different, and seemingly impossible, in a way that is properly structured and properly organized. This is why the approach we take here is both systematic and systemic. Structuring the initiative makes it systematic; involving many players across all levels of an organization makes it systemic. When executed in this way, an initiative allows organizations to harness change and use it as a competitive advantage, thus being able to respond quickly yet methodically to the transforming organization's needs. This method also allows you to maintain, and even increase, productivity and results throughout the entire time period, beginning when the organization initiates the change until it implements it on a full-scale basis.

An Inclusive and Systemic Model

Our model is "inclusive" in that it describes how to involve everyone who is affected by a change initiative and keep everyone across all levels of an organization informed of progress and problems. The model follows a distinct methodology of phases, and each phase includes inputs and outputs. The process also provides clearly defined roles and responsibilities for those who work directly with the initiative as members of a change steering committee.

The model looks at any change initiative from a "big picture" view and involves all parts of an organization that will be impacted. The communication aspect of the model is central and keeps dialogue and information flowing, decreasing the productivity loss that typically occurs when people are distracted by thinking about what might happen, or when they waste time huddling in small groups talking about what might happen.

We want to go further with this idea of inclusiveness and discuss why we think that a systematic use of an organization's resources is important to the ultimate success of a change initiative. Consider this question: Have people become so amenable to change that there is no need to emphasize the group, unit, or team aspect of the organization involved in change—and the resistance to it? We would say the answer is "no," especially when you look at the ill fate of many corporate changes that have been attempted in recent years. We believe that mobilizing people working together in a systematic fashion is an important component of ensuring that change initiatives work as planned. You are likely already aware that teams are built, not formed. Simply giving a group an assignment and putting them together in a room to solve a problem has not proven to be effective. A well-constructed team has the advantage over fragmented individual efforts because of the synergy it generates. One idea produces another; then that idea is expanded by someone else on the team and critiqued by others. Any idea generated among the team members is put to the strongest test, which results in the best possible path or solution to the tasks involved in the change.

Many great ideas failed because people did not bond and move toward a common goal. The old world order where competition was encouraged made it extremely difficult to move toward teamwork. Many people who thrived in the workplace under an industrial or manufacturing economy did not have, nor need, the skill set for cooperative learning and working. From infancy we are taught to compete. Our society encourages situations where one must win and one must lose. We rally around sports and talk of "winning" the game or "beating" the other team. But within every sport are teams that must work together toward a "common end." The "win-lose" situation might work well in sports and in businesses that require a competitive advantage over those who also seek the same customers. However, only a "win-win" situation within an organization will allow it to achieve its goals. Competition among groups or departments within a company only restricts growth. Internal competition stifles an organization's ability to move beyond the barriers and impasses that, if not addressed properly, cause the organization to fall behind in solving problems that prevent it from moving forward. In today's fast-moving business climate, there is no such thing as standing still. The moment you stand still, you begin to slip backwards.

The new world order, based on a knowledge and service economy, requires cooperation and synergy to truly succeed. We dedicate this book to proactively organizing people for a change initiative on a widespread basis within an organization, whether in groups, units, committees, or teams and whether permanent or temporary. The purpose of organizing people for change is to allow them to achieve goals that will move their organizations forward rapidly by implementing initiatives that will achieve their overall objectives. This will only happen by differentiating roles and responsibilities within units of an organization and giving those units the authority to make change happen.

Linking the Model to Productivity and Results

You are aware by now that the subtitle of this book is "an inclusive, systemic approach to maintain productivity and achieve results." We want to explain how the model you have reviewed in this chapter links to that subtitle.

One of the usual reactions to change initiatives is lower productivity, accompanied by decreasing morale and a host of other unfavorable factors. We know that employees react in these ways due to the uncertainty, stress, and chaos that usually accompany change.

We do not believe that loss of productivity and decreased morale during change are inevitable. An organization can execute a change initiative without experiencing these negative effects. We will settle for maintaining productivity and results after an organization jump-starts a change initiative, but our goal is actually to increase them.

The reason that we are so confident in this model is that it causes one to look deeply into the organization to determine the exact need for change. The model clearly allows you to identify "who needs to know what" in a manner that saves the organization time and money. Several parts of the model provide strong analytic tools to ensure that participants make optimal decisions and judgments about investments associated with the change initiative. The model maximizes input and sharing information among stakeholders throughout the organization, while the steering committee provides strong leadership along the way.

This model is far removed from chaos, uncertainty, impulsiveness, recklessness, and other problems that haunt change initiatives. We would not be surprised if an organization that follows this model carefully puts together one of its most productive and profitable time periods, even in the face of change.

Structure of the Book

This book is broken into four units: the first is introductory, the subsequent three represent components of our model: Unit 2 covers stakeholders, Unit 3 the process, and Unit 4 communication. Within each chapter are numerous tools to help you record information, make decisions, and advance through the process. We also provide two case studies that demonstrate the implementation of each aspect of the model by using issues that you can relate to. The first case study reflects an important cultural shift in an office services corporation that has changed the way that all of its departments access information by implementing the SAP process. The second case study is a health care organization that has completely realigned its organizational structure. The case studies are composites based on actual change initiatives that took place in similar organizations. At the end of each chapter, you can read a "slice" of each case study that applies to the material that we covered in the previous pages. We also include a section entitled "What Could Go Wrong" to highlight some potential problems and possible solutions.

The book is also accompanied by a CD-ROM that contains all of the tools from this book as well as the complete text of both case studies. You can use the tools in their current form or modify them to meet the specific needs of your organization or project. The CD-ROM also contains a PowerPoint® presentation that outlines the entire change model. It follows the structure of the book but, even more importantly, follows the structure of the change. The PowerPoint presentation can be used with the project team at the beginning of the Planning phase to overview the entire model. The slides can then be used again at the beginning of each phase to review that phase. The presentation can also be used to explain the process to (and enlist the support of) upper management, other impacted groups, and interested parties within the company.

Requirements for Change

1

Change and the Growth and Complexity of Organizations

OVERVIEW

OFTEN MID-SIZE OR LARGE ORGANIZATIONS begin as small operations, comprised of people who have a common understanding of their goals, along with their methods for conducting business. That commonality of interest and purpose is what likely drew them together in the first place. People communicate on a one-on-one basis frequently, regardless of the method: face-to-face, telephone, videoconference, or e-mail. This lack of complexity in the organization means that there is a high degree of centralization of authority residing in a few people, all of whom champion the common goal. You can probably think of several examples of huge companies with national prominence today that at one time were very small operations, such as Ford Motor Company, Microsoft Corporation, Dell Computer Corporation, and Ruth's Chris Steak House.

However, as the business enlarges because of its success, the organization brings on other people who do not necessarily share or understand its goals or philosophies. Without a mechanism to indoctrinate these new employees or partners, at a certain point of growth, the organization will likely experience a crisis. Profits may begin to fall, various parts of the organization may begin in-fighting, and the spirit of cooperation that was vibrant among the co-founders disappears. This erosion usually happens so slowly that, unless an organization is proactive (either because of great foresight or because it has been burned before), it will likely suffer at least a temporary decrease in productivity and profitability.

In the extreme, if organizations cannot react quickly enough, they may not recover at all—and could cease to exist. Since consumers now have widespread accessibility to services on the Internet, entire industries with companies that once prospered, such as travel agencies and walk-in music stores, find themselves in severe jeopardy. The proliferation of cellular phones has significantly decreased the availability of, and profits from, coin-operated telephone equipment. In small towns across America, many independent and privately owned businesses have surrendered to the massive buying power of superstores such as Wal-Mart.

Other changes do not happen fast enough. Between 1999 and 2001, many start-up companies, identifying themselves as "dot-com's," peppered the marketplace in all types of businesses and industries. They predicated their businesses on the enthusiasm generated by consumers who increasingly gained access to the Internet, and they believed that, over time, shoppers would exercise a preference to shop online, rather than in person or via a traditional catalogue. Most of these businesses did not have the available capital and financial resources to wait out the predicted shift in shopping styles and closed their doors, or more accurately, portals.

William Bridges (1991) suggests that some organizations that experience change never cleanly and fully break with the past. You may be aware of the struggles that organizations face in defining a new culture after two or more companies join forces as a result of mergers and acquisitions. Recent examples such as MCI and WorldCom, Hewlett-Packard and Compaq, and AOL and Time Warner illustrate the difficulties that employees face in working for merged organizations that have experienced massive change. In each of these examples, not only did employees have to gain familiarity with new or realigned products and services, but they also faced new cultural issues concerning the basic "way to work."

In many cases, the principal task for such an organization is to define an identity for itself, as well as for its investors and consumers. We are not surprised that Peter Senge (1990) stated in *The Fifth Discipline* that the life expectancy of a corporation is less than half that of the average human being.

In today's economy, changes occur so frequently that, where once an organization had perhaps a single major innovation in a decade to contend with, its business now requires it to balance several changes simultaneously, or one right after another. In the early 1990s, carbonated soft drink companies such as Coca-Cola and PepsiCo viewed beverages such as tea, fruit juice, water, and isotonic drinks as competitors and enemies. As we write this book, every major soft drink parent company in the world owns the trademark to one or more of these drinks, as their attitude has changed to "sell whatever we can." This evolution has produced massive challenges for practically every department in these organizations, including sales, marketing, and accounting, and challenges for external players such as suppliers, distributors, and retailers.

Some changes in an organization are highly dependent on other internal or external changes, so responses to each have to fall into place exactly on time, or there can be a backlog of missed deadlines and opportunities. Consider what happened in the first quarter of 2002, when the telecommunication industry faced unprecedented challenges that demonstrate this chain reaction of change. When consumers drastically slowed their purchase of cellular phones through retail outlets, companies such as Nokia, Ericsson, and Motorola slowed their production of these phones. When the production rates of phones declined, suppliers such as Texas Instruments (TI) slowed their production of chips to place in the phones. As TI reduced the number of chips it produced, it needed fewer employees, suppliers, vendors, and consultants. As a result, stock prices dropped, shareholders lost confidence, and related industries and organizations experienced pain. Every one of these organizations reacted in turn to changes produced by another organization.

Organizing Change

We believe that organizing change with properly built units, whether teams, committees, or departments, allows organizations to harness change and use it as a competitive advantage. By doing so, organizations are able to respond quickly, yet methodically, to a variety of needs. This inclusive approach maintains productivity and achieves results. Despite the challenges and circumstances an organization faces while experiencing change, using groups to produce and harness organizational change provides significant benefits that we speak of in this book. Throughout these pages, we detail the importance of an organization's change steering committee that drives a change initiative. Additionally, any department, division, or work group affected by a change initiative may assume the same proactive outlook in its day-to-day operations.

With change occurring so fast, employees in organizations have little or no time to recover from the preceding change. And how long does an organization have to make any one change? The answer is "as long as your customer and market will allow." Contemporary supermarkets truly flaunt "one-stop" shopping and include floral departments, banks, hardware, and gifts, in addition to traditional food and beverage. Jim Collins (2001), in *Good to Great,* explains that one grocery chain, A&P, chose not to make this transition and continued to predominately sell food items. Many of its stores have not altered in appearance or content since the 1950s. Modern consumers do not want to make five or more stops to save money. They want to make one stop and buy everything in one place and will pay higher prices to do so. The loss of customers and market share have truly squeezed A&P, and the chain has elected to move out of many markets.

Recognize that if your organization is the sole provider of a product or service, you have plenty of time to recover from any change, providing that the demand for your product or service remains high. The National Football League has maintained high resiliency in the face of several competing leagues since 1960, including the American Football League (with which it merged in 1969), the United States Football League (which folded in 1985 after two years of operation), and the XFL (which barely operated one season). Since the NFL is the only source for professional football, it has withstood changes in salary demands, television contracts, licensing agreements, and other potential downsides and has only encountered one work stoppage in its storied history.

But what if your customers can go elsewhere? Then you have very little time to organize for change. When McDonald's sold the only kids' value meal and possessed the only on-premise playground, it was the sole source for parents to go for these services. Today, every fast-food hamburger chain, including Wendy's, Sonic, Burger King, Carl's Jr., and Whataburger, offer special value meals for children. Business operates in a customer-driven environment. Customers expect services that meet their needs and are convenient for them, or they go where they can get what they want.

In summary, organizations must undergo change, whether they plan to or not. There is a significant advantage in organizing change and harnessing the competitive advantage that accompanies it. By using our seven-phase process, which we base on acting systematically, inclusively, systemically, and proactively, an organization can avoid the typical losses it might otherwise take in morale, productivity, profits, and other results.

In the next chapter, we describe the three parts of the model that we feature in the book.

2

Introduction to the Model

OVERVIEW

IN THIS CHAPTER, we introduce you to how our change model works and provide some information about its component parts. Henceforth, we use the term "model" when we discuss the interaction among three aspects: stakeholders, process, and communication. We use the term "process" when we discuss the seven phases of change. We use the term "initiative" to refer to any change project the organization chooses to undertake. In our model:

- *Stakeholders* are the agents that drive change initiatives (Unit 2);

- *Process* is the seven phases of change that an initiative proceeds through (Unit 3); and

- *Communication* is the vehicle the agents use to gather and disseminate information about the change initiative throughout the process (Unit 4).

Purpose of the Model

We believe that people resist change for four basic reasons:

1. Lack of involvement in the process;

2. Lack of knowledge about the change;

3. Insecurity about the future as a result of the change; and

4. Feelings of powerlessness to control their own destinies.

The model we present in this book can remove much of the pain that organizations face during a change initiative. The model that you read about here:

- Champions widespread involvement throughout an organization;

- Centralizes gathering and disseminating information;

- Provides a systematic, phase-by-phase process for change with defined roles and responsibilities; and

- Uses a change steering committee as the driving force to represent the concerns of all participants at all levels of the organization.

Overview of the Model

We assume that readers believe as we do—or that we can convince you of our belief—that change is inclusive, systematic, systemic, and proactive. The focus of the book is tactical and practical. There are many other books in the marketplace that show people how to manage, cope with, and deal with change. Very few works have attempted to harness and lead change in a proactive manner, and none with the systematic and systemic approach that we bring here.

We divide the model into three key aspects, each of which is a separate unit in the book: (1) Stakeholders, (2) Process, and (3) Communication. We have designed a three-dimensional diagram called a "cube" to demonstrate the interaction among these three key aspects (see Figure 2.1). Each chapter begins with a "slice" of the cube to ensure that you know where we are. Additionally, you can use the cube as an index to locate specific

Figure 2.1. The "Cube."

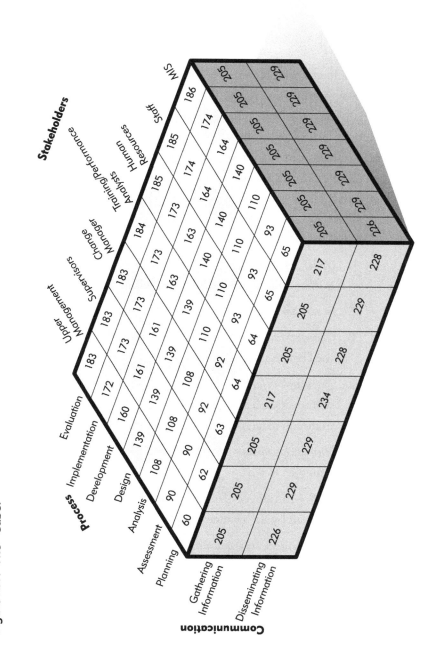

information that you need. For example, if your interest is in what a supervisor does in the Planning phase, the cube can direct you to the particular pages in the book that address those activities.

Stakeholders

Stakeholders are representatives from each affected group in an organization. Your organization may call them by different names, but their functions remain the same. Your initiative may not require all of these groups of stakeholders, but if you follow our model for determining the full scope of involvement, you will know which ones you need by the end of the Planning phase. We provide a general look at each group of stakeholders as the focus of Unit 2.

The various stakeholders we list, along with how to select them and their roles and responsibilities during each phase, are

1. *Upper Management*—Usually persons at the executive level who initiate or support the initiative with financial resources;

2. *Supervisors*—Line managers in charge of operational (staff) groups;

3. *Change Manager*—The manager who will drive the initiative and lead the change steering committee;

4. *Training/Performance Analysts*—Members of the educational group who oversee learning, knowledge, skill improvement, and performance management for the organization;

5. *Human Resources*—Members from the group who deal with employee issues;

6. *Staff*—Employees from the areas of the organization that will be affected by the change; and

7. *Management Information Services*—Members of the group that oversees the technical infrastructure of the organization.

In addition, you will find references in the book to the following:

• *Change steering committee*—The team that leads the change initiative in the organization;

- *Financial analyst*—A staff member who specializes in budgeting, cost/benefit projections, and return on investment (ROI);

- *Communication specialist*—A staff member who writes releases, memos, and articles about the change initiative for the organization, intranet, and media; and

- *Organization development analyst*—A person who specializes in analyzing the interaction of the change steering committee.

Change Process

The change process we discuss in this book assumes an enterprise-wide initiative. You can apply these same principles and methods to smaller initiatives by simply deleting and modifying the roles and responsibilities for your own division or work group. Our focus in the process unit is on the change steering committee as the team that organizes and drives the initiative forward. One of the features that makes our model inclusive is that there are opportunities for input from staff members, as well as the creation and involvement of various task forces, subcommittees, divisions, and departments. Only you can decide what is best for your organization. The change process we discuss in Unit 3 has seven phases:

1. *Planning*—Identify the issue to investigate and assemble the change steering committee;

2. *Assessment*—Determine whether there is a gap for the organization between the present state and the desired state;

3. *Analysis*—Decide on the means to bridge the gap;

4. *Design*—Configure the objective for the change initiative;

5. *Development*—Prepare everything for the change: the systems, the people, the materials;

6. *Implementation*—Put the plan into effect; and

7. *Evaluation*—Track and measure the effectiveness of the change.

The book provides tools for you to walk through and record information for each phase of the initiative and to track decisions and activities. You will also find these tools on the CD-ROM that accompanies this book.

Communication

The third component is Communication, discussed in Unit 4. Communication ties the entire model together. We believe that it is the central and most important aspect in the success of any change initiative.

The two elements that we discuss are

1. *Gathering information*—How you collect information, using fact-finding skills, interviews, and focus groups, and

2. *Disseminating information*—How you distribute information among change steering committee members, other stakeholders, and the overall organization.

In order for a change initiative to take hold in a successful manner, you must keep the members of the organization informed of all aspects of the project. While the process is complex, communication refers to how participants in an organization collect and disseminate information during the life of the change initiative.

Advantages of the Model

The major advantage of our model is its ability to help organizations to "get it right the first time," because for many change initiatives there is no second chance. Another advantage to this model is that you can apply the principles and methods to an organization-wide change as effectively as to a departmental or group change initiative. The time to complete a project will depend on the scope. If it is an enterprise-wide change, it will take longer than a departmental change. When you use our model, you will work hard, but you will find you spend less time backtracking and making corrections to previously completed activities.

Unit 2

Stakeholders

3

Change Agents

OVERVIEW

IN THIS CHAPTER, we focus on the various stakeholders who are actively involved in all phases of the change initiative. These stakeholders, or change agents, permeate all facets of an organization undertaking the initiative. We focus on stakeholders who are members of the change steering committee, which is the team that drives a change initiative forward for an organization. Recognize that emanating from the change steering committee, a variety of subcommittees, task forces, departments, and divisions can provide input and participate in execution of the initiative. Without a strong driver, such as the change steering committee led by an experienced change manager, the effort can be haphazard and costly. The change steering committee and change manager ensure that you undertake the change initiative in an organized manner. The first formal activity for both is the "kickoff meeting," which announces the fact that the organization will undertake a change initiative and rallies support from all employees for the subsequent phases in the process.

In Chapter 4, we follow up with some advice that you need to be aware of as you consider particular individuals for certain positions. In Chapter 5, we address issues related to committee members' interactions. In Unit 3, you will read about the specific roles and responsibilities that each of these stakeholders performs in each phase of a change initiative.

Duties of Stakeholders

The activities required for change management involve individuals at every level of the organization. As W. Edwards Deming stated in a video interview, *The Deming of America,* "Quality will not improve until you get the front line workers involved" (Petty Productions, 1991). Change must begin at each level of the organization. The process cannot begin at the top and then work down the organization. Neither can it begin with the front line people and work up. Groups must work with employees at every level simultaneously, providing information and training applicable to their needs and positions. This information and the training have as much to do with how they do their jobs as it does with their part in the change. This attitude is consistent with our premise that a group approach is the best vehicle to organize and effect successful organizational change.

Stakeholders are representatives of all affected groups. Each group must be involved in the decision-making process that results in change. Many of these stakeholders participate on the change steering committee, representing departments and divisions throughout the organization. The committee generally includes the following:

- *Upper management*;
- *Supervisors* from the affected areas;
- A *change manager* to lead the steering committee;
- *Training and performance analysts* who can determine the training needs for the new system implemented by the change initiative;

- *Human Resources* representatives who can work to determine the career ladders for those who will work on the new system and those who will transfer out;

- *Staff* employees who must adapt to the change initiative, but who also provide valuable input, including financial analysts and corporate communication experts; and

- Technical experts from *management information services* (MIS) who can evaluate the hardware and software components.

Additional members from the affected areas of the organization should be on the committee; however, their presence should not be so overwhelming as to sway the balance of the committee in any one direction.

We have systematically charted the responsibilities and activities of each of the participants by project phase in Unit 3 chapters (see Chapters 6 through 13). At this point, we will outline the general roles of the change steering committee members.

Change Manager

The change manager is responsible for coordinating the activities required to effect organizational change. This individual has the overall responsibility of steering the initiative forward, where the change, when implemented, becomes the "way the organization works." A change manager must be an expert in dealing with myriad focal points that he or she must juggle simultaneously, being sure that each piece falls into place at the appropriate time. The change manager must be certain that everything comes together when it is time for the change to be implemented and needs to make decisions from an informed basis when differences become difficult to resolve among his or her committee members. A change manager who is doing his or her job works to remove the obstacles from the paths of the change steering committee members, as well as from the members of all of the other subcommittees so that they can all perform their jobs.

The change manager should be accessible during all phases of the change process. In addition, the change manager should be actively involved in each of the activities of the change initiative. Only with a hands-on approach can the change manager know what is actually happening at each stage of the process. Participating in the required training provides valuable information—formally by "knowing" rather than just "knowing about" what is happening in each committee and informally through holding discussions with the committee members who contribute to the decisions about the change.

Upper management must always debate whether the change manager should be someone internal to the company or an external consultant. There are pros and cons to this issue, and each situation requires the consideration of different factors.

An external consultant as a change manager is likely to be quite objective in carrying out his or her duties. While the external consultant certainly has some history with the organization and its key players, in this role, he or she does not work directly for any specific department or division. Employees will view this change manager as relatively unbiased toward any actions that he or she will recommend for the change steering committee. In many cases, employees will also view the external change manager as more credible, due to his or her breadth of experience with several other organizations.

We have worked with and talked with companies who have hired external consultants that felt at the end of the initiative that perhaps they should have gone internal. An outside consultant, unless he or she is paid on the basis of the success of the change or guarantees a certain amount of savings (which is rare), does not have as much invested in the success of the change as an existing employee who will work there after the change is implemented and who has to face other people in the company. He or she may possibly have to sponsor or steer other change projects. However, if your company does not have the expertise in-house and cannot hire someone directly, you will have to use a consultant. The ultimate question is whether you have the expertise to proceed. This job falls to HR professionals who can scour your organization for candidates.

Here is the actual experience of one company we heard about that decided to use an outside consultant as change manager for a project:

A company that produced golf carts was getting a bad reputation because, six to eight months after they manufactured a cart, the bumpers fell off. The bolt that held the bumpers in place was a snap bolt that, once put into place, should not have been able to work itself loose. The company paid a very high-dollar manufacturing consultant to find a solution to the problem.

The consultant reviewed the designs and could find no problem. He finally went to the manufacturing floor and asked the assembly line workers why the bumpers might be falling off. The assembly line workers pointed out that they did not turn the bolt the entire distance (from 3 o'clock to 9 o'clock) because it scraped their knuckles. They only turned the bolt from 3 o'clock to 7 o'clock.

Since the bumper problem was not immediately apparent as the carts came off of the assembly line, the carts went to the field in seemingly good condition. An engineer would never have realized this problem because he or she never went to the floor.

The solution that the consultant suggested was to remanufacture the bolt at a significant cost to the company. The solution worked.

A few months after the consultant had been paid and the company had remanufactured the bolt, a supervisor thought to ask what the assemblymen thought of the new bolt. They all agreed that the redesign was much better because they no longer scraped their knuckles and could tighten the bolt completely. But one assemblyman commented, "I don't know why you didn't just give me an extension for my wrench."

This example shows that some of the best ideas may actually reside inside an organization, and that the use of an external source may be superfluous.

Upper Management

Upper management should openly express support of the overall change initiative and communicate the benefits to the company and to each individual employee. Upper management should also express confidence in the members of the change steering committee by empowering its members to make good decisions for the organization.

When the organization begins work on the change initiative, upper management needs to provide recognition of the efforts of the change steering committee for successfully completing a project and for achieving milestones along the way. Here is a list of what some companies have done to recognize the efforts of project committees.

For Successful Implementation

- Take the entire committee and their significant others on a vacation with all expenses paid.

- Give each committee member an all-expense-paid vacation for two.

- Let committee members share a percentage of the amount saved by the company during the first year as a result of implementing the change.

- Give each committee member a flat bonus.

- Have an awards dinner and ceremony honoring the committee members.

- Give awards, certificates, plaques, and other items.

- Promote committee members to positions of responsibility.

- Give raises or bonuses.

For Successfully Meeting Milestones

- Give committee members money to take their spouses, partners, or significant others to dinner.

- Sponsor an informal dinner for committee members paid for by the company.

- Have a pizza party during work hours.

- Give cups, caps, buttons, and other logo-identified items that celebrate the successes and call attention to them.

The key is to find out what will motivate the committee members and apply those rewards. Check all viable options and let the committee vote or even choose their own individual rewards.

Supervisors

Supervisors should express the benefits of the change initiative for their employees. These benefits include how this change will improve everyone's jobs and how each person will be more efficient and effective. The supervisors should also stress their role and discuss the ways that they plan to be involved in various facets of the change.

Perhaps most importantly, supervisors need to provide support for their employees as they work through the implementation of a change initiative. Not only should they answer questions, but they need to allow employees the opportunity to "vent" feelings and frustrations, as well as voice opinions and provide contributions.

Supervisors are key links in the inclusive nature of our change process. They should communicate input from employees to the proper members of the change steering committee. This is the only way that the organization can use its employees as a valuable resource for ideas. How many potential ideas have gone unused during a change initiative simply because no one heard or received them? Two of the key responsibilities that supervisors have is to ensure that the change steering committee receives employees' input and to insist on proper follow-up.

Staff

The staff members of the change steering committee should emphasize that they will have a significant role in decisions regarding the change and that they intend to represent their peers. All staff members throughout the organization should understand that they are encouraged to provide input through their representatives.

We recommend that three staff members with specialized skills participate on the change steering committee: A financial analyst, who can assist with budgeting, cost/benefit and return on investment calculations, a corporate communication specialist, who can coordinate the dissemination of information, such as releases, memos, articles, and postings on the corporate intranet, and a statistician.

Management Information Services

Technical personnel from management information services (MIS) should evaluate the hardware and software requirements if the change initiative involves or requires an installation or change in technology, which, in today's workplace, it usually does. Does an available system exist that meets the company's requirements? What are the requirements to build a customized system if such a system is unavailable? How durable and dependable are these systems? Will the chosen system fulfill the requirements needed to successfully effect the change? Technical experts in this department can determine which system is most durable and can be adapted to the unique needs of the organization. It is a mistake to choose a system and then adapt your business to it. The system is a tool. As such, the tool must *work for you*; not *you for it.*

Training/Performance Analysts

Training personnel should evaluate the learning and performance improvement interventions that are available for implementing a system required by a change initiative. These interventions may be a course, curriculum, an on-the-job (OJT) tool, self-study program, video-based instruction, Internet-based instruction, job aids, or a host of other options. If an intervention is not already available, training and performance analysts should develop the learning strategies so they are ready to use when the organization implements the change. If the strategies are commercially available, but do not meet your company's needs or quality standards, you may be able to work with the supplier to improve them and/or customize them for your organization.

At the kickoff meeting, all employees need to hear explanations from the change manager about how the training function will work in the change initiative. The assurance that employees will receive adequate guidance to do their jobs in new required ways will comfort them and will reduce some of the apprehension that they feel about the change. Employees in every department affected by the change need to be assured that they will receive the required tools. They also need to understand that, before the organization implements the changed system, staff members will be involved in evaluating those tools.

Training and performance analysts should also provide instruction on the various phases of the change process, since many on the change steering committee will enter the process without a clear understanding of it. This activity is critical to the smooth operation of the change initiative.

Human Resources

Human Resources (HR) has a big job. HR professionals must counsel employees about their future and manage a host of options to ensure employees that the organization will take care of them in some way. Often in the case of technological change, the possibility exists that there will be a reduction in staff. Employees anticipate this and, therefore, will become resistant. Insecure employees can sink a promising change initiative before it even gets started. Therefore, employees need to be reassured that they will not be sacrificed. There are many ways to do this. HR can reassure employees that plans are made up-front to look out for their interests. The cooperative nature of the company sends a strong signal to all employees that they will be taken care of in the event of a layoff and not just discarded. Interestingly, we are aware of several change efforts that actually required an *increase* in the number of employees rather than a decrease.

If necessary, a reduction in staff should first be accommodated through natural attrition, such as retirement or persons leaving the company. Second, those who choose to initiate a career change within the company should start immediately on their new career ladders. You may be surprised at how many employees in a department are willing to change jobs. Last, if people do need to be laid off because of the change, the company should arrange to help them make a positive career transition. Career counseling is a start, but continued financial support while they are retraining is also important. An example might be to provide tuition toward an education or training program for a certain amount of time after the person is laid off. You could determine the actual amount by examining the average tuition to trade schools and colleges in the community or surrounding area. You may want to be sure that each laid-off employee impacted by the reduction in force (RIF) receives some amount of time at an outplacement firm, where he or she can receive professional assistance from experienced career counselors, attend job-related seminars, and access important resources. Many companies provide this long-term support in one form or another through a severance package.

When people know they are not forgotten and that they have a real role in the decision-making process of the company, they can put personal issues aside and concentrate on helping move the change forward. A management team would be naive to think that employees should and will consider the company as their first priority. The days of the "company man" (or woman) are over.

Studies on work-life balance programs (Galinksy, Kim, & Bond, 2001; Litchfield & Pitt-Catsouphes, 1999; Smith, 2001) have shown that employees are willing to take a different view of their jobs, even to sacrifice promotion and money, if gaining these means sacrificing family and leisure time. This change of attitude might seem surprising in a business environment where downsizing has become increasingly common and jobs are harder to find, yet it is a fact.

Many companies have created vicious cycles where the very policy of staff reduction in hard times creates poor attitudes among the workforce during good times. Twenty-five years ago, when there were tough times in a company, people were kept on-board. IBM, for example, had a longstanding policy against layoffs. Job security was a reality. Today, employees have learned—usually the hard way—that if the company begins to lose money, their jobs may be sacrificed. The attitude is "Why should I do more than the minimum expected when, at any time, I can be shown the door?" Federal Express remains one of the few major companies that still retains the philosophy of the "social contract."

Everyone has heard of or has known someone in management who worked seventy hours a week for twenty-five years and was then let go. They missed seeing their families grow up and sacrificed any personal life to "get where they are today." And where is that? Often the attitude is to get as much out of a company as you can while you're there because you don't know how long the job will last. The enlightened company will take these issues into account and plan ahead. There is no more important time to conduct this planning and to take these steps then at the outset of a change initiative. Further, the "Gen-X" and "Gen-Y" populations that have entered the workforce have seen their parents laid off or seen the parent of a friend mistreated, and witnessed the hardships that follow. As a result, many of these employees are unwilling to sacrifice their lives for a company.

In the following chapter, we discuss ways that you can make effective selections for the participants on the change steering committee.

4

Choosing Committee Members

CHOOSING MEMBERS for the change steering committee and other subcommittees or task forces involved in the change process is one of the most important steps we discuss in this book. If you truly believe that a lack of involvement signals a lack of commitment, then the selection of people to serve on committees for the duration of a change initiative is a crucial responsibility and an action that the organization cannot make hastily. In this chapter, we provide some methods for making proper selections that will work effectively for you during your change initiative. We focus on the change steering committee, but the principles apply to other subcommittees or task forces as well.

The Nature of Committees

The change manager needs people with expertise in their fields to fill the seats on the change steering committee. Remember that the organization is its own socio-political group. Some people will work for the change, some will work for their own agendas, and others will not contribute at all. The best way to choose change steering committee members is to inspire them to volunteer. There can be no doubt that the best candidates to work on committees during the change process are individuals who are favorably disposed toward change and who succeed and thrive under situations that call for change. The change manager should clearly state the expectations and requirements of the function to be assigned when contacting a department manager with a request for him or her to assign some employees from that department to the change steering committee.

In some cases, department managers will assign employees to various tasks anticipated or necessitated by the change initiative. They may accomplish this by choosing people whose background and experiences best match the job to be performed. Everyone who joins the initiative should understand and accept from the beginning the philosophy that "only the project wins." As with many encounters, the focus should be on the issues, not the people.

Regardless of how you choose change steering committee members, the change manager should provide certain criteria ahead of time to the volunteers, both those assigned and their supervisors, to give them guidance about the type of people needed for the committee, above and beyond professional expertise.

Options for Selecting Members

In this chapter, we want to give you two options that can help you determine the best match between the available people and tasks required of them as members of committees. The first is based on research conducted on some longstanding characteristics of innovative people. The second is based on our observations in organizations and best practices of change-oriented individuals. Again, these options work for both membership on the change steering committee as well as for any subcommittees or task forces that the organization decides to enlist during a change initiative.

Individual Rating Method

Bill Lee has developed a questionnaire (see Exhibit 4.1) based on the personality, communication, and socioeconomic characteristics of innovative people as identified by Everett Rogers (1983). For optimal effectiveness, both the employee who is a potential committee member and his or her supervisor should complete the checklist. The change manager should score the checklists (using Exhibit 4.2, which should not be provided to the raters) after they are returned and before he or she interviews the potential committee member. The change manager should use the completed questionnaire as a guideline while interviewing each potential committee member. Only those employees who receive a passing score should be interviewed.

Interviewing Method

Co-author Karl Krayer has taught and used the behavioral interviewing method in various organizations. Behavioral interviewing is based on the premise that past behavior is the best predictor of future performance.

We have printed a list of potential questions for a behavioral interview below. Recognize that this list represents the lead, or first, question. You will need to decide whether to probe for additional information depending on the quality of the answer you receive. All of these examples are adapted from actual interview questions that managers have used to select participants for positions of responsibility on a significant project in an organization. Following each question, we have placed the change principle that the question addresses.

"Please describe how you handled a recent situation where you were not sure what expectations someone had whom you either worked with or for."

- Principle: High tolerance for ambiguity
- Principle: Works well around others who are inconsistent or unpredictable

Exhibit 4.1. Innovation Checklist.

Name of individual being rated: _____

Date: _____

Rater: _____
(Your responses will be kept strictly confidential.)

Rate the individual by placing a plus (+) next to each item that accurately describes him or her.

_____ 1. Displays high degree of empathy for others.

_____ 2. Admits errors in thinking when presented with facts.

_____ 3. Discusses abstract ideas with understanding.

_____ 4. Supports assertions with proof or documentation.

_____ 5. Demonstrates intelligence on the job.

_____ 6. Readily accepts change.

_____ 7. Remains positive when faced with uncertainty.

_____ 8. Expresses a favorable attitude toward information derived from research.

_____ 9. Does not accept imposed changes as inevitable.

_____ 10. Initiates ideas for change more often than others in a similar position do.

_____ 11. Participates in social and professional organizations and in company social activities.

_____ 12. Demonstrates concern for how the actions of his/her own department affect other departments.

_____ 13. Attends business and professional meetings outside of the immediate geographical area served by the company.

_____ 14. Is involved in political and/or social organizations that work toward change.

_____ 15. Avidly seeks sources of information (newspapers, magazines, television) on business, professional, and social issues and discusses them with colleagues.

_____ 16. Communicates effectively in one-on-one situations.

_____ 17. Regularly brings information about ways to improve the department or business organization to the attention of peers and supervisors.

_____ 18. Speaks about potential improvements in a manner that demonstrates that she/he has conducted research on the topic.

_____ 19. Others listen to his/her opinions.

_____ 20. Volunteers or is often chosen for interdepartmental committees or task forces.

_____ 21. Is widely read (business, professional, leisure).

_____ 22. Has highly specialized skills rather than a general knowledge of many things.

"Explain the way that you made adjustments to a long-term project that seemed to constantly change in one way or another."

- Principle: Ability to work under turbulent conditions

"Tell me about how you participated in a recent meeting where you met with others to make a decision or solve a problem, particularly as compared to the way that the other group members participated."

- Principle: Ability to contribute

"Discuss the feelings you experienced and how you outwardly behaved when you participated in a meeting that exceeded your expectations and that you perceived was of high quality and worthwhile."

- Principle: Optimistic and excitable

"Explain the steps you took to complete a recent project that did not have clearly defined methods, requirements, milestones, or timetables."

- Principle: Able to complete projects that are not clearly defined

"Describe the way that you felt when you accomplished a task well, but did not receive overt recognition or appreciation for what you did."

- Principle: Ability to forego personal recognition and appreciation
- Principle: Team-oriented

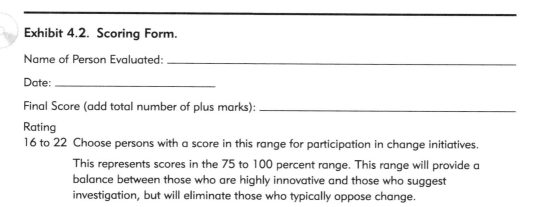

Exhibit 4.2. Scoring Form.

Name of Person Evaluated: _____

Date: _____

Final Score (add total number of plus marks): _____

Rating

16 to 22 Choose persons with a score in this range for participation in change initiatives.

This represents scores in the 75 to 100 percent range. This range will provide a balance between those who are highly innovative and those who suggest investigation, but will eliminate those who typically oppose change.

Acceptance   YES   NO

As with any interview that uses behaviorally based questions, you must allow the respondent sufficient time to gather his or her thoughts and provide a coherent answer. Remember that these questions depend on the recollection and communication of past behavior as the best predictor for future behavior. They do not ask for hypothetical responses, conjecture, or speculation. As such, these answers are not typically "top-of-mind." Quality answers often depend on quality time to draw on the experiences that the answer requires.

Once the committee members are selected, your job is not yet done. You will likely need to spend some time learning more about the members and how they interact, as well as helping the members to get to know one another. Interaction issues are the subject of the next chapter.

5

Analyzing and Improving Committee Interaction

OVERVIEW

AFTER YOU HAVE SELECTED the change steering committee members, the change manager has the responsibility of organizing the committee. As is typical with groups as they begin to interact, you will likely find the members floundering around a bit as they get to know one another and as they get used to one another's communication styles and ways of operating in formal meetings. An objective analysis of the committee's interaction will reveal certain strengths, opportunities, and skills that the members can develop that are important to effective group functioning and making good decisions. Remember that you likely have assembled many forward-looking people on the change steering committee who have a positive outlook on change. They have ideas that they are excited about and would like to implement. Everyone can benefit from knowing how to participate in meetings that are as efficient and effective as possible.

Interaction Styles

Most likely, within the change steering committee are members with very different personalities and very different communication styles. Some are very aggressive and are willing to push hard for their ideas. Others are less aggressive and want to consider all the data and look at all sides of an issue before making a decision. Others are the diplomats who intervene as the negotiators for the committee.

All of these interaction styles are necessary in order for the committee to function well; each complements the others. Groups such as these thrive on differences, not on similarities. However, differences also complicate managing the committee. The change manager must monitor the interaction of group members to prevent interpersonal differences from harming the progress of the project. There are systematic ways of monitoring the group dynamics of a committee.

To evaluate the interaction styles that people use in groups, we have chosen to adapt behaviors and roles from Kenneth Benne and Paul Sheats' (1948) classic model. Their work has stood the test of time and, in addition to making distinctions between different personality types and their group interaction styles, it gives you a way to objectively analyze a group. The roles are distinct and clear. Each role corresponds reliably with predictable communication behaviors. The behaviors and roles are not difficult for a rater to analyze nor for a user to interpret and understand.

Additionally, while most group analysis methods focus on the leader of the group, Benne and Sheats recognized that each participant plays roles and that each person should be aware of his or her role, whether it is making a positive contribution or blocking group progress.

Group Membership Roles

Benne and Sheats divided membership roles into three classifications:

1. *Task Roles*—Roles that move the group forward to a solution to a problem.

2. *Maintenance Roles*—Roles that help the group members work together more effectively.

3. *Individual Roles*—Roles that exist to satisfy an individual's needs. The corresponding behaviors are not group-oriented and actually work against the productivity and cohesiveness of the group. The emergence of these roles always signals a need for group self-analysis. Identifying these roles may require some formal group training in group interaction. In some cases, simply identifying them for participants may be sufficient to produce a change.

Benne and Sheats subdivided these three role classifications into twenty-four categories, outlined in Table 5.1. We have adapted some of the descriptions for this chapter.

Table 5.1. Interaction Roles in Groups.

No.	Classification	Behaviors
	Task Roles	
1	Initiator/ Contributor	Suggests new ideas or group problem-solving strategies. Suggests a new group goal, new definition of the problem, new solution, or some way of handling a difficult situation that the group has encountered. Proposes new procedures or new ways of organizing the group.
2	Information Seeker	Asks for clarification in terms of facts or authority to support the problem under discussion.
3	Opinion Seeker	Asks for clarification, but is not concerned with facts as much as the values pertinent to the problem that others include in their assertions or suggestions.
4	Information Giver	Clarifies assertions by providing facts with the authority to substantiate those assertions.
5	Opinion Giver	States beliefs about how a suggestion fits with values of the problem or of the group, rather than about the facts.
6	Elaborator	Spells out suggestions with examples or attempts to give meaning to suggestions of others. Provides rationale for ideas and suggestions and explains how the ideas and suggestions would work if adopted.
7	Coordinator	Shows or clarifies the relationships between various ideas and suggestions, tries to pull various ideas and suggestions together, or coordinates the activities of various subgroup members.

(Continued)

Table 5.1. Interaction Roles in Groups. (*Continued*)

No.	Classification	Behaviors
8	Orienter	Summarizes for the group what has happened and points out departures from agreed-on direction or goals or raises questions about the direction that the group discussion is taking.
9	Evaluator/ Critic	Questions the practicality or logic of accomplishments by comparing them to a set of standards for completing a task.
10	Energizer	Prods the group to action or a decision or tries to stimulate or arouse the group to the highest quality activity or solution to the task.
11	Procedural Technician	Performs routine tasks such as distributing materials, coordinates the setup of displays or audiovisual materials, or rearranges the seating to help the group move forward as effectively and efficiently as possible.
12	Recorder	Performs the "group memory" role by writing down group discussion, decisions.

Maintenance Roles

No.	Classification	Behaviors
13	Encourager	Agrees with and accepts the contributions of others; provides warmth and solidarity in his or her attitude toward others; offers commendation and praise; indicates understanding and acceptance of others' points of view, ideas, and suggestions.
14	Harmonizer	Mediates differences between others, attempts to reconcile disagreements, or relieves tension in conflict situations through humor or by smoothing over disagreements.
15	Compromiser	Operates from within a conflict when his or her idea is involved. Offers to yield to others' positions, admits errors, disciplines self to maintain group harmony, and meets others at least halfway.
16	Gate Keeper/ Expediter	Keeps communication channels open by encouraging or facilitating the participation of others or proposes regulation of the flow of communication by limiting the length of time that any one person can hold the floor.

Individual Roles

No.	Classification	Behaviors
17	Aggressor	Deflates status of others; expresses disapproval of the values, acts, or feelings of others; attacks the group members or the validity of the problem; jokes aggressively; or shows envy toward another's contributions by trying to take credit for them.

Table 5.1. (*Continued*)

No.	Classification	Behaviors
18	Blocker	Behaves in a negatively and stubbornly resistant fashion, disagrees and opposes contributions without or beyond reasonableness, or attempts to maintain or bring back issues after the group has rejected or bypassed them.
19	Recognition-Seeker	Calls attention to self through boasting, reporting, or personal achievements. Acts in unusual ways and works to prevent self from being placed in an inferior position.
20	Self-Confessor	Uses the group to express personal, non-group-oriented feelings, insights, or ideologies.
21	Playboy	Displays lack of involvement in the group's processes in the form of cynicism, nonchalance, horseplay, and other overt or immature forms of behavior.
22	Dominator	Asserts authority or superiority by manipulating group members through flattery, and communicates superior status or the right to attention. Gives directions authoritatively and interrupts the contributions of others.
23	Help-Seeker	Attempts to get sympathy from the group by expressing feelings of insecurity, personal confusion, or self-deprecation.
24	Special Interest Pleader	Speaks as if he or she represents certain special-interest groups, rather than claiming ownership of the value or idea. Masks his or her prejudices or biases.

From K. Benne & P. Sheats. (1948). Functional Roles of Group Members, *The Journal of Social Issues,* 4(2), 41–49.

Rating and Analyzing Interaction
Rating Information

If you (or another independent rater) wish to use this typology to analyze the change steering committee's interaction, you must practice in order to become an expert in identifying actions and behaviors for each of the categories. Of course, you could use these roles and behaviors to analyze any subcommittee or group working on the change initiative. You should try this first in a group where you are a passive member, a listener, or otherwise not very actively involved. It is too difficult to try to analyze the statements made by others and at the same time think about what you need to say or do regarding the task or problem under discussion. You will be surprised how quickly you have to categorize the contributions each member makes. Simply listen to each person's input and then put it into the proper category. You may use "tick marks" or any other method that helps you keep up with the interaction. When the committee has finished its meeting, or the portion of the meeting that you are analyzing, you will have captured the number of statements made by each person in each category, which you may wish to convert to percentages for analysis.

The two principles that govern interaction analysis are exhaustivity and exclusivity. The principle of exhaustivity states that the tool has a category for any contribution that any member makes. The principle of exclusivity states that the tool has only one category that you can use for any contribution that a member makes. Or as you may remember your mother telling you as you grew up, "There is a place for everything, and everything has its place."

You may elect to have a training/performance analyst who is not part of the change steering committee, but who is well-versed in interaction styles and communication techniques, use this tool. If you choose to have an objective rater serve in this way, he or she should present the results to the entire team and review the findings with them. He or she can also suggest some intervention techniques or skill adjustments that can help the committee work more effectively. In addition, each member can review his or her own personal findings and talk with a training/performance analyst about options for improvement.

Your careful preparation will result in a successful analysis. First, make a seating chart of the group you are analyzing. Next, place a number corresponding with one of the twenty-four categories beside the name or position on the seating chart every time a person makes a contribution to the discussion. You should also try to jot down a few words of the contribution to help you remember what the participant said that caused you to categorize the statement in the way that you did. You may wish to begin a new sheet at time intervals, such as every ten or fifteen minutes, or as the agenda moves from item to item. Alternatively, you could use a table like the one shown in Table 5.1 and note each speaker's initials next to the appropriate role for each statement.

You will want to practice the technique on another group in a meeting before facing the pressure of capturing and interpreting data for the change steering committee. Before then, practice analyzing a script of statements such as the one in Exhibit 5.1.

Exhibit 5.1. Practice for Analyzing Interaction Roles.

Instructions: Use the interaction roles list in Table 5.1 to analyze the following script from a group discussion. Simply read each contribution and attach a category to it. You can compare your judgments to the set of correct answers that follows.

_____	Amanda:	"Yesterday we didn't have time to complete our discussion on which software package to buy. We need to make a decision, so let's go back to that discussion."
_____	Rita:	"I've been doing some research and found that there are two that have all of the capabilities we need."
_____	Bob:	"Why do we have to use some sort of computer software to do this? Why can't we do it by hand and save a lot of money?"
_____	Dominique:	"Bob, if you take into account the amount of man-hours expended on doing this by hand, the software pays for itself in less than three months."
_____	Juan:	"But how much time is really expended?"
_____	Roberta:	"And is the process being done as efficiently as it could be?"
_____	Perry:	"I think it is."
_____	Joe:	"I think there is a lot of waste in the present process."
_____	Perry:	"Do you have any data to support your position?"
_____	Joe:	"Yes. I have looked at the data for the past year and compared the amount produced to the number of hours charged directly to the work. It's way out of line."
_____	Perry:	"Joe, I think you're way out of line. I do that job and I think I am the best person to judge that."
_____	Sally:	"Well now, Perry, sometimes the person closest to the process can't see the inefficiencies."
_____	Mary:	"Let me give you an example of where I think that time could be saved in the process."

(Continued)

Exhibit 5.1. Practice for Analyzing Interaction Roles. (*Continued*)

———— Ken: "I'll be glad to set up the computer and load the software."

———— Amanda: "Thanks, Ken."

———— Alicia: "I think that we should use the most effective and efficient method possible to accomplish this administrative stuff. That will leave us more time to do the major tasks."

———— Randy: "It seems the major task of this group is to discuss things but never get anywhere."

———— Samantha: "That's not fair, Randy. We have made a lot of progress."

———— Amanda: "All right, all right. Let's try to stay on the topic and not get into personalities."

———— Randy: "That's assuming that people in this group have personalities."

———— Pam: "OK. What we've decided so far is that there is some lost time and that software would do the job better and quicker; it is cost-effective."

———— Raul: "If that's true, then what are we waiting for? Let's make the decision."

————Karen: "Yes, let's vote."

Your Analysis

Instructions: Analyze the various interaction styles of this committee. We have included some suggested answers on the following pages.

1. What is the most frequently used interaction style?

2. Who assumes the task roles most often?

3. Who assumes the group roles most often?

4. Who assumes the individual roles most often?

5. What would help this group function better?

Exhibit 5.1. (*Continued*)

Answers to Group Interaction Scale Activity

8	Amanda:	"Yesterday we didn't have time to complete our discussion on which software package to buy. We need to make a decision, so let's go back to that discussion."
4	Rita:	"I've been doing some research and found that there are two that have all of the capabilities we need."
18	Bob:	"Why do we have to use some sort of computer software to do this? Why can't we do it by hand and save a lot of money?"
4	Dominique:	"Bob, if you take into account the amount of man-hours expended on doing this by hand, the software pays for itself in less than three months."
2	Juan:	"But how much time is really expended?"
2	Roberta:	"And is the process being done as efficiently as it could be?"
5	Perry:	"I think it is."
5	Joe:	"I think there is a lot of waste in the present process."
2	Perry:	"Do you have any data to support your position?"
4	Joe:	"Yes. I have looked at the data for the past year and compared the amount produced to the number of hours charged directly to the work. It's way out of line."
22	Perry:	"Joe, I think you're way out of line. I do that job and I think I am the best person to judge that."
14	Sally:	"Well now, Perry, sometimes the person closest to the process can't see the inefficiencies."
5	Mary:	"Let me give you an example of where I think that time could be saved in the process."
11	Ken:	"I'll be glad to set up the computer and load the software."
13	Amanda:	"Thanks, Ken."
5	Alicia:	"I think that we should use the most effective and efficient method possible to accomplish this administrative stuff. That will leave us more time to do the major tasks."
18	Randy:	"It seems the major task of this group is to discuss things but never get anywhere."
5	Samantha:	"That's not fair, Randy. We have made a lot of progress."
14	Amanda:	"All right, all right. Let's try to stay on the topic and not get into personalities."
17	Randy:	"That's assuming that people in this group have personalities."
8	Pam:	"OK. What we've decided so far is that there is some lost time and that software would do the job better and quicker; it is cost-effective."

(*Continued*)

Exhibit 5.1. Practice for Analyzing Interaction Roles. (*Continued*)

10	Raul:	"If that's true, then what are we waiting for? Let's make the decision."
11	Karen:	"Yes, let's vote."

1. What is the most frequently used interaction style?
   Task Roles
2. Who assumes the task roles most often?
   Perry and Joe
3. Who assumes the group roles most often?
   Amanda
4. Who assumes the individual roles most often?
   Bob and Randy
5. What would help this group function better?
   Only one person in the group is process-oriented. The other members focus only on the task. The group needs to add more process-oriented people to the group or ask one or more of the other task-oriented members to assume a process role. If you choose someone from the group to assume the process role, choose someone who is not contributing as strongly to the task.

Analyzing Interactions

As a debriefing for the analysis, and after you have collected sufficient information, share the twenty-four categories with the members of the group and discuss each category to be certain that each member understands what the category means.

In your analysis, you can look for issues such as:

- What is the percentage of contributions in each of the three areas (task, maintenance, individual) for the entire committee?

- What is the percentage of contributions in each of the three areas (task, maintenance, individual) for each committee member?

- What is the percentage of contributions in each category of behavior for the committee? For each member?

- How did the categorization of contributions change as the meeting progressed over time?

- How did the categorization of contributions change as the committee progressed from topic to topic on the agenda?

Once you and the change steering committee have complete understanding of the twenty-four categories and their use as well as their value to the group, provide each person, individually and privately, the data that you collected. Offer to discuss the data with individual members after the meeting.

What if all of the members of the change steering committee do not approach you to discuss their data? If they exhibit individual behaviors that are detrimental to the committee's functioning, then you should seek them out on a personal basis to discuss your findings.

What happens if the analysis reveals an overabundance of roles in either the group maintenance or group task categories and too few in the other? In that case, you probably need to give an overall summary of the data, and the group may need to discuss the need to either add other members to the group or ask for group members who would feel comfortable filling the roles of those categories that are weak. Usually a group of sufficient size, say twelve, will have enough people who naturally play certain task or maintenance roles. Remember that most people usually play more than one role in a meeting.

We think there is great value in correlating the results with the topic under discussion, as well as with the timeline for the discussion. As the committee continues to meet, the members can learn to adapt their interaction styles from topic to topic. For example, one topic may be quite emotionally charged, with members contributing more individual role behaviors than on other topics. Perhaps that is the time for someone on the committee to "step up" and provide maintenance behaviors. On another topic, the committee may be very high in "opinion giving," but very low in "information giving," thus indicating the need for additional research, facts, and data. What does it say about the committee if there is only one member who "seeks information"? And what if another member continually "gate keeps," but never gives information or an opinion?

You will be surprised by how excited members can be about interpreting and analyzing their own results. In some cases, all members need to do in order to get motivated about improving their work on the committee is to see these findings, especially as they may change over time.

Note: This type of analysis works as well for the groups outside of the committee that members have to interact with. You can quickly determine whether someone is cooperative toward the change or whether he or she has an intention to block it.

Now that you're familiar with the makeup of the change steering committee and have learned about group interaction issues, it's time to look at the process for the change initiative.

Unit 3

Process

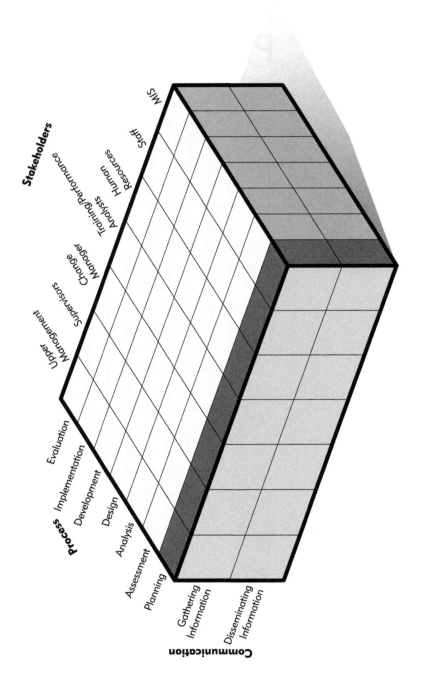

6

Planning

IF AN ORGANIZATION wants to achieve the results and productivity it desires from implementing a change initiative, proper planning is essential. In this phase, the organization identifies its change manager, who begins the process of overseeing the entire initiative. One of the first steps that he or she takes is to seek out other change steering committee members and define each person's roles and responsibilities.

Note that in the Planning phase, members of the organization feel some discomfort and uneasiness in the way that it operates due to a problem, condition, threat, or circumstance. Perhaps a new competitor's tactics have cut into sales and profits, or a dated distribution system produces an inefficient route to market, or a new legislative edict requires modifications in its advertising and promotions. At the outset of this phase, the organization has not made any decision about whether to introduce a change initiative. One of the most important activities in this phase is for key members of the organization

59

to discuss whether they share these feelings of discomfort or uneasiness and, if so, whether it is important enough to proceed with some sort of formal initiative to change them.

Inputs

The input to the Planning phase is the recognition that there is an issue or opportunity within the organization that requires investigation. This can be any issue, ranging from one that affects the entire organization to one small group that provides influence within the organization.

Outputs

The output of the Planning phase is a fully formed change steering committee, led by a change manager, that is ready to function and solve the problem or meet the opportunity.

Responsibilities/Activities

Table 6.1 graphically depicts the tasks that have to be completed by the time the change steering committee is formed.

Upper Management

Upper management must interview prospects for, and then hire, the change manager. They then need to charge him or her with the responsibility to form the change steering committee and empower him or her with the authority to plan and effect the change initiative. Upper management must also provide and commit the financial resources required to complete the project, as well as support mid-management in changing the operating schedule to release people to serve on the steering committee and other department members throughout the organization to assist in the initiative. The organization cannot expect employees who are not involved in work authorized by the change steering committee to pick up the work left by people who are involved. However, a "rousing" speech at the kickoff meeting about everyone "putting in a bit more work now for the common benefit later" should help.

Table 6.1. Responsibilities During Planning.

Planning

Upper Management

- Hire change manager
- Charge change manager with responsibilities and authority
- Commit to financial and human resources for the Planning and Analysis phases of the project
- Communicate the "felt" rationale for the change
- Preside at kickoff meeting
- Present united front to employees

Change Manager

- Coordinate completing the Project Management Tool
- Coordinate kickoff meeting
- Organize change steering committee
- Charge change steering committee with roles and responsibilities
- Provide project overview (milestones, goals) to the change steering committee
- Consult with financial organization on the cost/benefit of solving the issue and maintaining budgets
- Preside at kickoff meeting

Human Resources

- Review the nominations for change steering committee members

Management Information Services

- No specific responsibilities in this phase. All responsibilities covered under Shared Responsibilities

Supervisors

- Recommend change steering committee members
- Complete tool selected for nominating staff for membership on the steering committee (see Chapter 4)

Training/Performance Analysts

- Provide training on teambuilding skills
- Fact-find for needs on team building (interpersonal skills, knowledge of the change process)

Staff

- Represent peers by presenting their questions and concerns

Shared Responsibilities

- Complete the Project Management Tool for this phase
- Attend kickoff meeting
- Communicate with peers

Upper management must clearly formulate a felt rationale for the change, describing how the initiative will positively impact the company, for example: "The executive committee believes that our company is losing market share because we lack the technology we need for efficient automation." Employees will not be committed to the process, and they will likely resist if they do not understand why the company is undertaking the initiative. The employees may not agree with the rationale for the change, or with the initiative itself, but at least they cannot say that they did not have the rationale explained to them.

Upper management must also present a unified front to the change steering committee and all affected employees. Total agreement may not exist among members of upper management. If so, they need to resolve any differences that remain. This allows the employees who are affected by the change to perceive a strong commitment among the most visible members of the organization who are responsible for strategic and tactical planning.

All of these management responsibilities must be communicated to employees at the kickoff meeting, which we detail in Chapter 14. At this meeting, held just before the Assessment phase begins, the CEO presents a keynote speech. Upper management introduces the members of the change steering committee and emphasizes their confidence in the capabilities of each individual.

Supervisors

Supervisors should recommend staff members from their functional areas for the change steering committee. Those who supervise supervisors should also recommend supervisors for the committee.

Upper management should ask supervisors to complete the analytical tools we provide in Chapter 4 on each individual they recommend. As a courtesy to those employees the supervisor recommends, each person should receive a blank copy of the checklist to let them know the criteria on which they are to be evaluated. The employee who is the focus of the evaluation should have the option of stating whether he or she wants to have the checklist completed on himself or herself. If someone objects, the supervisor should not complete the checklist and should initiate a search for another person who is qualified to serve.

Note: Sharing the evaluation criteria with the prospective change steering committee member is especially important in a union environment. The change manager should fully explain the procedure to union management, along with the purpose and use of the form, in order to obtain their agreement.

Change Manager

The change manager is responsible for many of the activities that officially "kick off" the change effort. These include coordinating the initial change steering committee meeting, organizing the kickoff meeting, providing the steering committee with its initial roles and responsibilities, and offering a complete overview of the entire change initiative. This overview may include the projected date of completion, agenda for meetings, and general goals. The change steering committee may further refine these goals during the Assessment and Analysis phases, but the committee should see the layout of the project and have a general idea of what upper management expects of them. The change manager must also coordinate completing the Project Management Tool, assigning roles and responsibilities to all participants for this phase (see Exhibit 6.1).

The change manager must work closely with the financial organization for two reasons:

1. To assist in establishing and maintaining the budget for the initiative, and

2. To determine the cost/benefit ratio of the project that the solution will bring as well as the return on investment (ROI) after the initiative.

Note: Although each staff committee member is not specifically named, other than as affected stakeholder groups, we assume that a member of the financial organization will be assigned to the initiative to assist the change manager in maintaining budgets.

Training/Performance Analysts

As we stated in the Introduction to this book (and bears repeating here), "Teams are built, not formed!" This is a critical but often forgotten fact. In order to function in an optimal way, the change steering committee should operate as a team. That is where training comes in. There are a large number of team-building courses and books available. Any group, committee, unit, department, or division needs to practice the principles and skills that define good teamwork.

Any good course or reference book on team building for a change initiative will:

1. Present material that the consumer can view or read in a short period of time;

2. Include skills that are relevant to teams working on a change process;

3. Provide steering committee members with tools to work through issues, barriers, and tasks together; and

4. Address barriers to effective teamwork.

The agenda for all project meetings undertaken by the change steering committee should include an overview of any team-building activities, principles, or training programs. These are particularly impactful for the first few meetings that the change steering committee holds.

Human Resources

Human Resources should begin to search internally for those persons who have expertise in the subject matter that is the focus of the issue or problem driving the change initiative. For example, if an organization realizes it is losing money because it is a solely corporate-owned rather than a partially franchise-owned operation, there may be employees who have worked for other companies that made a similar change. If HR does not currently have a list of the capabilities of people within the company, they should begin a survey to compile one. If an internal search comes up empty in any area, then an external source should be sought for that stakeholder group.

Staff

The staff who work with or for members of the change steering committee are critical. In many cases, the change steering committee will contain one representative each from a variety of departments. The staff, working with the change steering committee member, come from the groups that will actually accomplish the work required by the change initiative. The staff actually have a finger on the pulse of the issue that is under consideration. They must be the link between the steering committee and their peers—to answer questions and raise issues in the committee that must be considered and resolved.

Management Information Services

All groups that might possibly be needed for the initiative should be included in the Planning phase, although each group will not have specific responsibilities during each phase. This is the case for management information services during Planning.

Shared Responsibilities

All change steering committee members should participate in completing the Project Management Tool (see Exhibit 6.1) for this phase. The committee typically accomplishes this at its first meeting, although they may require more time to work through it. All change steering committee members should also attend the company kickoff meeting and be prepared to explain what their roles will be on the steering committee. All members should begin to talk about the planned change to those they represent, even if they do so only in general terms.

Assigning Roles and Responsibilities

For the initiative to be successful, everyone must have a clear understanding of his or her roles and responsibilities. We recommend a Project Management Tool like the one in Exhibits 6.1 and 6.2 to organize the assignments for the initiative. We have had success with projects where this matrix was implemented because it identifies who is responsible for making the decisions or accomplishing tasks on each and every aspect of the project. You may have used a similar tool if you have worked on project planning for another purpose.

The Project Management Tool

During the first change steering committee meeting, the change manager should provide a general overview of the entire process for all the committee members. The change manager should have completed a draft of the tool for each role to be filled at the outset of each subsequent phase, but the entire steering committee must work as a team to further define the roles and responsibilities and to be certain that the correct group and correct persons have been assigned the roles and responsibilities. The Project Management Tool is a dynamic document that the committee updates throughout the initiative.

The change steering committee can complete the tool as follows:

1. The change manager should provide each member of the change steering committee with a blank tool (see Exhibit 6.1).

2. Everyone should complete the Project and Phase information.

3. The committee should place the names of each member of the steering committee across the top in the "name" row just under the Project and Phase.

4. The change steering committee should brainstorm all of the roles that are required for the initiative during the current phase.

5. The committee should reach consensus on roles that should be included and any that are redundant and should be excluded.

6. Once the necessary roles are determined, a role should be assigned to each person in the "name" row and entered in the "role" row below the person's name.

7. The committee should brainstorm a list of all the tasks that are required to be completed during the Planning phase.

8. The committee should reach consensus on tasks that should be included and any that are redundant and should be excluded.

9. The committee members list each task on the left side of the matrix under "tasks."

10. Each change steering committee member should complete the worksheet independently, assigning the task to the person he or she thinks most appropriate using the following criteria:

    • Place an "R" under the name and beside the task for the person who should be *responsible* for the task. The person responsible has the decision-making authority to ensure that the task is completed. There can only be one R per task.

    • Place a "C" under the name(s) and beside the task for the person(s) who must be *consulted* for the task. The person(s) who must be consulted are those who can add vital input or whose areas will be most impacted by the task. They carry out tasks that are impacted by what is done on this task. There can be as many C's as necessary to complete the task.

    • Place an "I" under the name(s) and beside the task for the person(s) who must be kept *informed* about the progress or status of the task. There may be more than one I per task. They are typically those who have an R under their name for related tasks, but are not directly impacted by another task.

11. The change manager should tally all of the responses under each task. The person who receives the most nominations for each task should be the person responsible for that task. These tallies will likely engender some conversation among change steering committee members. The committee members should be certain to review the entire tool for consistency. For example, the members will want to ensure that the person responsible for one task is consulted or informed on tasks that are interdependent.

Note: Sometimes this matrix includes an "A" for *accountable* in order to distinguish between the person responsible for the task and the person who is accountable for carrying it out. We believe the person who is responsible should also be accountable. Having two people in that role subtly relieves the accountable person of responsibility and removes his or her authority to make decisions. Having to continuously consult with someone else to gain his or her permission may unnecessarily hinder completion of the project.

In the completed example in Exhibit 6.2, J. Kemp is responsible for developing observation instruments. J. Black, R. Roy, and K. Levy are the team members for this task. They must keep all the other team members informed because they are working on other activities. B. Lee must be kept informed because he is the change manager and has to report to upper management.

K. Su is responsible for validating observation instruments and S. Martinez, R. Roy, and K. Levy are the team members. All other members must be kept informed because validation impacts all other tasks. Again, B. Lee must be informed also. And so it goes with each of the other tasks.

Remember that while the change steering committee members may complete the tool for the entire project at the first few meetings, they must revisit the tool as the committee enters each new project phase. Completing one phase of a project may make the members realize that there are more tasks in subsequent phases than they originally thought.

Benefits of the Project Management Tool Approach

We are all flattered when others ask for our opinion and, of course, we feel obligated to give it. However, an opinion can be taken or ignored by the person asking for it. Our experience has been that when someone asks for your opinion, he or she is really seeking confirmation or affirmation for his or her own idea. If you tell the person what he or she wants to hear, the person will go away happy and implement the idea. If questioned, the person can always say, "Well, Bill agreed with me."

Exhibit 6.1. Project Management Tool.

Project:					Phase:			
Name								
Role								
Tasks								

R = Responsible　　　C = Consulted　　　I = Informed

Exhibit 6.2. Sample Completed Project Management Tool.

Project:	Telecommunications				Phase: Analysis			
Name	J. Kemp	S. Martinez	K. Su	J. Black	R. Roy	K. Levy	K. Krayer	B. Lee
Role	Analyst	Analyst	Analyst	Analyst	Analyst	Analyst	Editor	Manager
Tasks								
Develop Observation Instruments	R	I	I	C	C	C	I	I
Validate Observation Instruments	I	C	R	I	C	C	I	I
Conduct Observations	I	I	I	R	C	C	I	I
Summarize Data	I	I	I	I	C	C	R	I
Write Audience Analysis Report	I	R	I	I	C	C	I	I

R = Responsible   C = Consulted   I = Informed

If you don't give others the answers they want, they go to the next person on their mental list and ask their opinions. This continues until they hear the answer they want. If they don't get the answers they want, they may implement their own ideas anyway, with the reasoning being: "Well, I asked six other people and they all gave me different opinions, so obviously, they can't agree either. That makes my option just a good as theirs."

With the Project Management Tool approach, the correct response when someone asks for your opinion is to take out the tool and identify the person responsible. The agreement seekers don't give up easily if they can still get someone's affirmation other than "Mary's," but when they get that response enough times, they finally give up and just go to "Mary" first. This saves a lot of time.

Case Studies

As we stated in the Introduction, at the end of each chapter in this unit, we present slices from two case studies that will help make the description of each phase come alive for you. You can read the entire text of both case studies on the CD-ROM that accompanies this book. At the end of each chapter, we present some issues and concerns that you may encounter during the phase that you have just read about.

The first case study details the way that an office service organization changed the way that its employees could access information for greater effectiveness and efficiency. The second case study explains the way that a health care products organization enacted a change by totally restructuring all aspects of the company.

CASE STUDY 1
BACKGROUND

Many organizations have felt the effect of decreased efficiencies and effectiveness due to redundancies in task procedures, job functions, and routine processes for conducting work. In addition, many employees find routine job responsibilities difficult to execute because they require travel through multiple levels of authority and responsibility.

In order to eliminate these problems, companies have eagerly endorsed data warehousing systems, such as SAP. The company, SAP, founded in 1972 in Walldorf, Germany, produces a product, also called SAP, that allows an organization to compare key processes and key players, eliminating singular functions performed by multiple employees, and allowing employees "real time" access to company data that formerly were reserved for, or controlled by, a select few.

One of the major benefits to installing SAP in an organization is to increase efficiencies. Most companies only allow certain employees to obtain particular types of information, such as sales figures and budget status, among others. If other employees in the organization need data that they are not authorized to access, they have to obtain the information through a third party. This procedure can result in considerable delays, particularly when some of the "gate keeper" sources are out of town, on vacation, sick, or otherwise unavailable. The delays can result in late reports, lost sales, improper forecasting, lost credibility with customers, inaccurate projections, and other problems that hurt business. Once a company installs SAP, the system allows real-time access by several sources to data, thus allowing decision making to proceed, reports to be generated, issues to be investigated, and forecasts to be more accurate. Note that an SAP system still allows an organization to make decisions and enforce regulations to control access to data, but not at the expense of efficiency and effectiveness.

A company's implementation of SAP affects many different processes at many different levels of the organization, thus changing, if not overhauling, the work of a great number of employees. Because the system reduces redundancies, an organization may also reassign or eliminate employees, throwing many departments or divisions into initial chaos and creating widespread change and all the challenges that accompany it. On the positive side, implementing SAP also allows for job enrichment and job enlargement for employees. An organization can expect more from individuals when they perform their jobs with the tools provided by SAP.

The transformation to SAP is the problem we take you through as we watch change progress. This is a significant cultural shift for the organization, Blumroth Office Systems, a parent company with 2,800 retail outlets throughout North America, with 72 percent of the stores franchised and the remainder company-owned. The corporation sells office-based products of all types in a warehouse-style atmosphere, and it also employs a number of business consultants with expertise in a variety of industries. Profits for the current year to date are up 7 percent over the previous year, and the company has posted profits for three consecutive years. Blumroth is privately owned and has been in business for five years. Approximately 850 employees work at the corporate headquarters in Atlanta, Georgia.

PLANNING

At Blumroth there is a great deal of disagreement over the direction that the company should take regarding teamwork versus specialization. The company has been very slow to adopt the notion of cross-functional teams; most departments and divisions work in specialized silos. The atmosphere is friendly and collegial, although not particularly cooperative. When one group needs information or resources from another, such assistance is a low priority, with each department preferring to handle its own business first. Many of the employees at Blumroth have spouses or friends who work in a more team-oriented climate, and this provides a rather uncomfortable comparison for most of them when they discuss work in off-the-job settings.

About six months ago, the chief executive officer (CEO) of the firm, Frank Adams, expressed his displeasure about how long it takes and how many organizational levels one must go through to get the information necessary for some employees to do their jobs. In some cases, by the time that a user obtained the needed information, it was already outdated. Frank formed a users group with a cross section of employees representing a wide variety of departments in the company to investigate how widespread and significant this problem actually was for the business. He made it clear that the group was not solving a problem, but just discussing whether a problem even existed.

Frank formed this group after receiving data from a number of exit interviews with employees, as well as from some conversations with colleagues from other organizations. At some professional meetings, he heard about SAP. He personally investigated the merits of SAP, not only by obtaining their literature, but also by meeting with various company representatives. However, Frank made it clear to the group that he was not pushing any preferred solution and, in fact, never mentioned SAP during the meeting.

After listening to employees talk about their jobs throughout the company, there was no question in his mind that backlogs in various processes in many departments were the rule, not the exception. Frank called members of his executive team together, shared the results from the users group, and asked each person to share his or her feelings about the issue. Following a subsequent meeting with other members of upper management, Frank believed that he had enough information to institute a formal investigation of the problem, leading to some potential change in the future.

To manage the change initiative, Frank named Jess Albertson, one of the original directors at Blumroth and a fourteen-year business veteran. Jess began his career with American Express Financial Services as a consultant and is now the senior vice president of marketing for Blumroth. His business acumen is considerably above average, although he has no personal experience with SAP or, for that matter, any other data warehousing solutions. He is well-respected throughout the company.

Jess set about the task of forming his change steering committee by requesting the names of people who were forward-looking individuals from every department that either accessed or requested any type of data for any job process or function. Each committee member was recommended for the committee by his or her immediate supervisor and was personally interviewed by Jess for participation. The committee represents highly diverse status levels throughout the company.

Committee members were selected from headquarters, as well as from retail stores scattered throughout the United States, and were brought to company headquarters in Atlanta to serve on the committee. These store managers would commute back and forth from their home bases to headquarters to communicate information to their peers. A video teleconferencing system was already set up in the company to accommodate company-wide meetings, so the store managers would sometimes join in meetings via the teleconferencing network.

Let's meet the committee right now. The departments they are affiliated with appears in parentheses:

• Jess Albertson—Change Manager—Senior Vice President (Marketing)

• Bill Duncan—Technical Analyst (MIS)

• Teri Anderson—Supervisor (Accounting)

• Henry Cisterian—Vice President (Retail Sales)

- Joy Kendall—Senior Analyst (Finance)

- Lee Franklin—Vice President (Advertising)

- Betty Richardson—Supervisor (Shipping and Mail)

- Steve Barry—Program Manager (Training/Performance Analysis)

- Hal Nelson—Manager (Corporate Communications)

- Benjamin Harold—Manager (Brand Marketing)

Once the committee was formed and Jess had met with the members individually to review their roles and responsibilities, Jess set the date for a kickoff meeting. At the first change steering committee meeting held just two weeks before the kickoff, Jess introduced the team to the Project Management Tool and outlined the various phases involved in executing a change initiative. Of course, the committee did not know any specifics about what would eventually transpire with the initiative, nor any form that it would take, but Jess was still able to suggest some milestones for the various phases. Jess also announced that he would work with Joy, who would take the lead on conducting cost/benefit analyses and establishing budgets, as the committee learned more about their task.

Frank Adams introduced Jess at an all-employee kickoff meeting at the headquarters building of the company. All of the senior management at the company were present at the meeting and expressed their support and enthusiasm for reviewing and investigating current business practices and processes at Blumroth. Frank noted that he did not know whether the organization would make changes, nor what form or direction those changes might take, but said that Blumroth wanted to be proactive and organize a team to prepare for a different way to work. Jess spoke to the employees for about ten minutes, during which time he introduced the members of his change steering committee and laid out an eighteen-month timetable for how the committee would work. He urged all employees to cooperate with the change steering committee and noted that there would be plenty of opportunity for each employee to provide input and get involved with any decisions that the organization would make. Due to the amount of uncertainty that existed at the time, employees asked very few questions and received very few answers.

Of course, initially, the steering committee members were filled with uncertainty and apprehension about the task ahead of them. Fortunately, Jess provided the direction that was necessary to start the initiative moving. From the beginning, he stressed the need for the change steering committee to operate as a team. Eloise Hardage, one of the corporate training/performance analysts at Blumroth, attended the meetings as an outsider to provide the necessary skill building in team dynamics and to provide Jess with feedback on his facilitation skills. Her input was well-received by the committee members. Over the next three meetings, each committee member worked to define his or her roles and responsibilities.

Once the steering committee members got to know each other and went through initial team training and task clarification, they approached the initiative with confidence and enthusiasm. Both of these attributes are important for success in the second phase, Assessment.

CASE STUDY 2

BACKGROUND

In an era in which many organizations have emphasized efficiencies in doing business, employees must "do more with less." At the same time, organizations place an increased emphasis on teamwork, collaboration, shared or cross-functional projects, matrix alignments, and skill application, while showing decreasing concern with job specialization, job titles, individual functioning, individual work histories, and territory protection. Part of this change is due to how many organizations now provide services rather than manufacture goods. Another contributing factor is that contemporary organizations employ workers from diverse backgrounds in many locations throughout the world. Many diverse cultures hail the "team" over the "individual" and, thus, managers now seek input from employees and emphasize cooperation among workers rather than deploying command-and-control techniques. Finally, organizations find themselves pressured by "speed-to-market" and quality requirements to keep one step ahead of their next competitor.

Not surprisingly then, organizations continually attempt to retool their operations and procedures in order to work in the most efficient and productive way possible. One of the most popular manifestations of this retooling is the continual evaluation of the way they align and organize their people.

One of the most popular ways that organizations accomplish "more with less" is by having employees perform numerous functions and activities in a cross-functional or matrix style. A matrix organization is formed by merging two of the following functions: territory, product, or customer. The case study you are about to read involves the transformation of an organization that has realigned its employees and functions from a traditional to a matrix system.

Northcutt Health Solutions is a privately held North American corporation that offers four primary services to three types of health care organizations. Northcutt manufactures products made of (1) paper, (2) gauze and cotton, and (3) polyethylene film, as well as (4) a complete line of printed materials for health care offices that they may use "off the shelf" or customize by having Northcutt embellish with logos, names, or other information. The three types of health care organizations that the company does business with are medical, dental, and veterinary. One of the largest divisions of the company is under "medical" and focuses on products for food service, including hospital cafeterias and patient service.

Some examples of paper products include those used for examination tables, gowns, caps, drape sheets, and all types of tissue. The company manufactures more than one hundred varieties of gauze and cotton products, most of which are bandages. Northcutt offers multiple types of polyethylene film, all of which are renowned for their strength and durability, and many of which are bags used for removal of raw material or waste or sealed for storage. The printing division includes catalogues and custom products, such as business cards, announcements, stationery, patient appointment cards, patient record forms, and a host of other items for medical, dental, and veterinary offices. The food service portion of the medical division produces all types of paper products for food storage, preparation, and service that are designed to meet or exceed local and state food safety regulations for personal protection.

Northcutt has its international corporate headquarters in Kansas City, Missouri. It has three manufacturing plants and five distribution sites. The corporate headquarters houses all of the administrative offices, along with manufacturing and distribution facilities. The company has a traditional organizational structure, with "silos" for each of its four products. Each product line is led by a senior vice president, and each contains its own field salesforce, marketing department, finance and accounting operations, and human resources. Within each silo, the field salesforce is organized into four zones: north, south, east, and west. The four silos share access to single corporate departments such as information technology (IT), package engineering (PE), new product development, supply chain management, office services, legal, payroll, graphic design, training and development, and maintenance.

The last three years have been challenging for Northcutt, which fluctuates from being number 2 to being number 5 among its North American competitors in market share and profits for its four products. Because the health care market is challenging and volatile, some of Northcutt's competitors have introduced innovations that have produced positive gains, while others have failed and been abandoned. The company pays its employees just below the national average for more than 75 percent of benchmarked positions, but its benefit package consistently rates in the 85th percentile nationally. A recent employee survey indicated above-average satisfaction with the job, company, and management. In spite of these results, senior management of the company revisits the way that it uses its resources and aligns itself on a semi-annual basis. Participants thought that last week's meeting was among the most contentious ever held, and almost everyone felt that there would be some type of shakeup announced within the next quarter.

The change you are going to read about involved a significant realignment of resources at Northcutt, including a reduction in workforce. Practically every job in the organization felt some effect from the change.

PLANNING

The impetus for the organizational change in this case study was an executive staff meeting held at the end of the first quarter of the year. As the CEO, Bruce Franklin, reviewed year-to-date results for the company as well as for competitors, he could feel some uneasiness in the room. He decided that he would call a special session for the team for the purpose of conducting an unofficial, highly opinionated session wherein each person could discuss a wide variety of issues about the company. The team met for this purpose three weeks later at an off-site location beginning on a Friday afternoon and continuing until Sunday at noon. The entire executive team attended, along with two high-ranking directors in finance and two trusted business consultants who had worked with Northcutt for several years.

After participants contributed to the discussion, the group unanimously agreed that continued fluctuations in market share, volume, and profits were quite risky. One member remarked that, as CEO, Jack Welch had turned around General Electric by declaring that unless the company was number 1 or number 2 in a product line, it would no longer make that product.

On Sunday, the team agreed that it would move in the direction of changing certain aspects of the way the company did business that would give it a competitive advantage. At this point, no one knew what to do, the extent to which the organization would make changes, nor the impact on results, but everyone knew that the organization would initiate something rather than stand still.

The final point of business at the retreat was to decide on the person to lead the organization through whatever change it would make. The team discussed candidates and decided that the best leader would be one of their own who was present at the meeting and who would be a strong advocate for the change. This person was Cherie Davis, who had a nine-year history with Northcutt and who was currently serving in her tenth month as vice president of new product development. Through the years at Northcutt, she had worked in five different positions, and employees considered her one of the most visible and forward-thinking associates in the company. She readily accepted the position of change manager and noted that her first duty would be to find an internal replacement for her own position to ensure that current projects continued forward without interruption. The team decided that the CEO, Bruce Franklin, would announce the new project, the rationale, and goals and announce Cherie's new position and responsibilities along with a promise of upcoming information in a company-wide e-mail on Monday morning. Everyone left exhausted by the magnitude of the topics they had covered at the session, but also feeling invigorated with the possibilities that the change presented for renewal.

As you might expect, the e-mail on Monday morning declaring Cherie's change in position to "change manager" sent waves of rumors and discussion running throughout the company. Many employees ran to their managers to see what they knew, which, of course, was little or nothing. Some managers even "rolled their eyes upward" at the thought of a new bureaucratic position entitled "change manager." Upper management had underestimated the rumor mill and the feedback. They realized they should have provided more information initially, so they sent out another e-mail explaining the project to the extent that they could. This helped quell the rumors, and Cherie realized very early that she needed a communication specialist on the project team and a communication vehicle to disseminate information. She decided to use the company intranet, which all internal employees had access to at every location.

Cherie interviewed two director-level employees in new product development and chose Tim Hardesty, a three-year veteran in the department, to replace her as vice president. Cherie told Tim she would announce this position change when the company held its change kickoff meeting toward the end of the Planning phase.

Cherie next set about the task of finding members for the change steering committee. She sent an e-mail followed by phone calls to various vice presidents and directors in the company to request the names of people in their areas who could responsibly serve on the committee. Bruce asked three of the Human Resources vice presidents to personally screen the recommendations and send finalists for interviews with Cherie. Since the committee would be fairly small, Cherie decided to interview each person personally. Bruce and Cherie wanted to ensure that everyone involved understood that participation on the change steering committee was in addition to, not a substitute for, his or her usual duties and responsibilities. As the process began, everyone was impressed that the recommendations reflected highly diverse status levels throughout the company. Cherie began these interviews immediately, including some by telephone and videoconferencing for those not at headquarters.

As a result of her interviews, these are the other members of Northcutt's change steering committee:

• Lois Hanratty—Software Support Supervisor (Management Information Systems)

• Melanie Farve—Supervisor (Supply Chain Management)

- Marcia Allen—Division Sales Manager (Printed Goods)

- Joe Churchill—Associate Marketing Manager (Gauze and Cotton)

- Harold Bekins—Associate Corporate Counsel (Legal)

- Marv Curtis—Senior Training/Performance Analyst (Training)

- Sue Davis—Senior Corporate Recruiter (Human Resources)

- Hugh Bennett—Vice President (Finance)

- Lynn Turvein—Manager (Corporate Communications)

Bruce consulted with Cherie on a Monday afternoon and they decided to hold an all-employee "kickoff" meeting two weeks from that Friday to formally introduce her and the other members of her change steering committee. They also decided to videotape the presentation and send copies to each employee who did not work at the headquarters and to establish a monitored chat room to answer questions as quickly as possible.

On Monday of the week of the kickoff meeting, Cherie met with her change steering committee for the first time as an intact group. She was upbeat in her mood, thanking them for their commitment to the company by volunteering to serve on this committee. Cherie ensured that members got to know each other a bit, and then she turned to an overview of the Project Management Tool for the initiative, a discussion of the cost/benefit analysis and budgeting, then to the business of the agenda for the kickoff meeting. She made sure that everyone understood the committee's purpose and expected outcomes (to be number 1 or number 2 in each product line), along with their roles and responsibilities. She also contacted all of the senior management team that participated in the decision to ensure that they would attend the kickoff event on Friday and, in some cases, to discuss certain roles and responsibilities with them. Cherie asked as many of them as possible to attend a walk-through of the event on Thursday afternoon. All but two of them were able to attend.

Cherie met with the two consultants who attended the special weekend session. They suggested that this kickoff meeting have a positive, upbeat atmosphere, with music, refreshments, balloons, clowns, and magicians, along with buttons and posters touting the theme "Help Us Find the Way." The idea was that everyone who attended should leave realistically understanding that the organization would change and that there was a lot of work ahead to determine exactly why and how. The intent was also for everyone attending to agree that fluctuations in market share and profits were a very unhealthy position for the company and that making a change was the right thing to do, even if no one could specify the exact nature of the change. They decided that the kickoff meeting should send the message that the company would change, but it would do so in the right way, after receiving and analyzing the right facts. The meeting would enlist everyone's support and cooperation, if not their enthusiasm.

The kickoff meeting began at 10:30 a.m. in the corporate training center. Many of the employees approached the entrances with uneasy or even low spirits, but their mood quickly changed on being met at the door by the clowns, who gave each person a button and brochure with the theme prominently displayed. The participants entered listening to upbeat music, and most of the senior management officials were present to circulate throughout the room to talk to employees as they munched on cookies and drank soft drinks or coffee. The lights lowered and a loud siren accompanied by blue and white strobe lights quieted the crowd. From behind a cloud of smoke, Bruce Franklin emerged and welcomed the group with great enthusiasm in his voice. After giving words of welcome and outlining the purpose of the meeting, Bruce introduced Cherie.

Cherie provided the rationale for the project. She explained that, over the next few months, everyone would have a hand in determining what was happening in the company and why. She stressed that there might be change and said that the change steering committee would need everyone's input about what that change might be.

Cherie then announced the purpose and role of the change steering committee and encouraged all employees to work with them whenever requested to do so. After introducing each member, she assured the employees that all facets of the company could provide inputs to the committee and that they were to feel free to contact any member at any time. She also charged the employees with the responsibility of providing the committee any information it needed in order to assist them in doing the work for the company over the life of the change initiative. She stressed that this is how each employee would be involved in designing the future of the company. She offered no time frame for how long the entire change process would take, but she did make it clear that the work would begin immediately.

Cherie closed the meeting by inviting Bruce and other senior managers back to the front to take questions from the group. Some employees asked if the forthcoming change for the organization could impact job security, layoffs, financial incentives, and other self-serving factors. A few employees asked follow-up questions about the organization and their jobs. Of course, there were no answers to these questions because they were all highly speculative. Bruce invited the employees to stay and mingle as they chose and stated that he, Cherie, and other senior managers would stay around to visit informally with those who wanted to do so. The entire meeting took less than one hour.

Cherie called her second meeting of the change steering committee just one week after the kickoff meeting. The meeting was typical of any early gathering of a new group of people who wondered why they were there and what they were to do. A few remarked that they did not want to appear to be traitors by participating in a process that their colleagues may actually oppose and, perhaps, be adversely affected by. Cherie stated that any of these concerns were totally speculative since no one had made any decisions about what the organization would be doing other than to stabilize market share and profits for the four product lines.

Cherie went out of her way to be prepared for this meeting. She gave packets to each member that gave them complete information and resources necessary to do their work well. She reiterated the importance of the Project Management Tool and provided an overview for each phase of the project and described the basic tasks that the committee must accomplish to complete the work. She emphasized that the committee needed to operate as a team and, at all times, present a united front to the organization, although she said that it was perfectly acceptable for everyone to discuss and disagree within committee meetings. Using the phases of the change process outlined in this book, she presented her best estimates of the upcoming timelines and milestones for the project. Cherie introduced Lynn Davis, one of the organizational development specialists for the company, who attended for the purpose of analyzing the group interaction (using the tool presented in Table 5.1). Lynn had agreed to attend as many early meetings as possible in order to provide some tips and techniques to help the group function effectively. Since all of the members of the change steering committee also had other responsibilities within the company, everyone appreciated using the time for their meetings in the most effective way possible.

Cherie then distributed updated copies of the Project Management Tool to each committee member, including items that the committee had discussed at its first meeting. Prior to this meeting, she had already updated a number of the tasks that the committee must complete, or see completed, for each phase on the draft of the matrix. She spent the remainder of the meeting asking the group to brainstorm all of the potential tasks that they could think of that belonged to each phase. There was some disagreement about whether certain tasks belonged in one phase or another, and Cherie helped steer the discussion. Obviously, the further down the line the phases went, the less specific the committee could be at this stage of its work. She also noted that within two days each committee member would receive an updated Project Management Tool containing the input from the discussion that day. She asked each member to review the matrix and add or delete tasks prior to the next meeting so that they could come to a consensus on assigning roles and responsibilities. Cherie announced that one of the first tasks the committee would undertake at the outset of each stage would be to review and update the Project Management Tool for that stage.

Cherie announced that, prior to the next meeting, she would meet with Hugh and other analysts from Finance in order to explore an initial budget and proposed return-on-investment figures for the initiative for everyone on the committee to review. She asked that each committee member return to his or her respective work areas and bring back any questions, concerns, or issues that required a committee response.

The committee met one week later, and Cherie was pleased with the way that the committee members completed their homework and were ready for and excited about the meeting. Lynn shared some observations based on the first meeting and ran the group through a brief exercise about productive conflict. She opened the session by taking input from members who brought issues and questions out of their respective areas. In some cases, she provided answers herself. In other cases, she asked the committee for input. Sometimes, she marked the question or issue as one that required widespread publicity, including posting on the corporate intranet, where Cherie had established a new section devoted entirely to the "Help Us Find the Way" theme. She also distributed copies of the budget and preliminary ROI projections and took questions from the committee members.

Cherie devoted the remainder of the meeting to discussing the Project Management Tool input, paying special attention to the section for the next phase, Assessment. The committee clearly disagreed about some issues, but was able to reach consensus on the tasks they must complete during the phase and who should work on each task. In several cases, the committee decided that it needed to defer to company resources outside their own group, and Cherie agreed to enlist the support of those employees' managers to assist.

What Could Go Wrong

Since these processes involve organizational change, you will likely encounter some barriers and obstacles. Everything about the change initiative will not go as you want it to, much the same as a football team is not always able to execute a play the way that a coach draws it up in the locker room. Following are some issues that may arise during the Planning phase for which contingency plans should be developed, each followed by a potential solution:

Problem: Qualified employees whom you really want to participate refuse to serve on the change steering committee.

Solution: The change manager or another influential member of the steering committee should explain the importance, benefits, and visibility that participation could yield for the individual. In addition, the employee has the opportunity to provide significant input to the role and responsibilities that his or her position will undertake once the organization implements the change initiative.

Problem: The kickoff meeting does not leave the employees in high spirits and excited about a change initiative.

Solution: Change steering committee members should divide various departments among them and conduct brief on-site follow-up meetings. Listen, receive input, answer questions, and reassure the employees that the organization will not forget them.

Problem: The CEO pushes a preferred solution rather than allowing the change steering committee to fully assess and analyze the situation.

Solution: The CEO has the authority to take this action, but the change manager should advise him or her about the need to gather data and follow the actions outlined by the various phases in the process. The change manager should explain that short-cutting the process by announcing a solution prior to a proper assessment and analysis could cost the company time and money.

Problem: Members of the change steering committee do not receive group interaction feedback in a constructive manner, and some appear offended.

Solution: The training/performance analyst or organization development professional who interprets the results should discuss constructive items in general terms with the team and then, if it is appropriate to provide constructive feedback to an individual, he or she should do so privately.

Problem: The CFO is not cooperative in releasing necessary funds to properly budget for a change initiative.

Solution: The change manager should ask the CEO to speak with him or her, and as with all persons affected by the change initiative, should involve the CFO and offer the opportunity to provide input.

Problem: The CFO refuses to discuss cost/benefit or return on investment (ROI) data without knowing the specific change initiative the organization will undertake.

Solution: The change manager should explain that no one has any idea what the exact initiative will be in the Planning phase, but without some preliminary input on these financial issues, the initiative will not progress efficiently. The CFO can discuss available funds and examine potential targets for cost/benefit and ROI without knowing specifics of the change initiative.

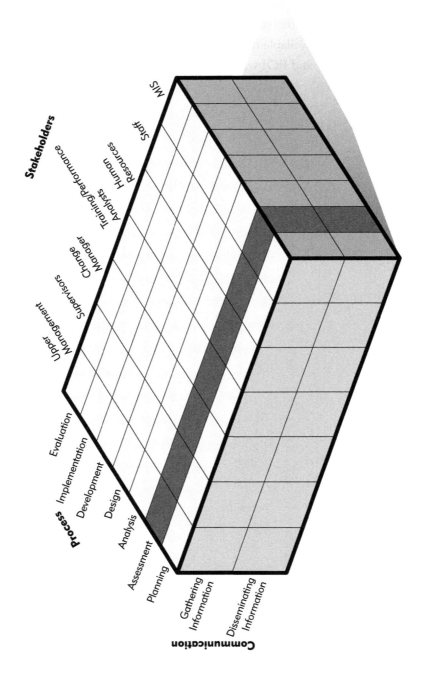

7

Assessment

IN THIS PHASE, you learn where you are now and where you need to be. Keeping in mind the organization's vision and mission, the change steering committee explores all of the facets of the current and desired situation. This chapter presents how to identify the gap between where the organization is currently regarding an issue, problem, or opportunity and where it wants to be after it fully implements a change initiative.

Inputs

The input is a fully formed change steering committee, led by a change manager, that is ready to function and solve the problem or meet the opportunity.

Outputs

The output from the Assessment phase is a report that fully explains the situation as it exists and what the situation should be in order for the organization to achieve its goals.

Responsibilities/Activities

Table 7.1 outlines the responsibilities of each of the stakeholders during the Assessment phase.

Upper Management

In this phase, upper management provides a vision for the organization. They create a vision statement that defines what the organization wants to "be" or "achieve" as a result of solving a problem identified in Planning. The statement should be simple and inspirational.

Here is an example of a vision statement:

Our vision is to become the world's leading company in the manufacture and delivery of professional moving products.

In a later section in this chapter, we present an associated mission statement, developed by the change steering committee members.

Supervisors

Supervisors need to examine operating schedules and provide their employees the time to participate in the change initiative. Major decisions include how to fill in for an employee who is serving on the change steering committee or on any dedicated subcommittee or task force so that service does not turn into punishment for the committee member or other employees who might have to take on extra work. Remember that, in addition to their committee work, members still have some or all of their own work-related

Table 7.1. Responsibilities During Assessment.

Assessment

Upper Management
- Provide vision statement
- State the criteria for successful change based on corporate goals

Change Manager
- Coordinate completing the Project Management Tool
- Coordinate activities of the steering committee
- Establish, monitor, and maintain the schedule
- Coordinate company and committee meetings
- Assist upper management in establishing vision and mission statements
- Present assessment report to upper management

Human Resources
- Monitor Assessment phase

Management Information Services
- Provide input into technological measures for assessment
- Select data analysis tools
- Assist in analyzing assessment data

Supervisors
- Provide employee time and relief from other responsibilities to participate in the change initiative

Training/Performance Analysts
- Coordinate instrument development
- Teach components of Assessment phase
- Assist in administering, collecting, analyzing, and interpreting results
- Write assessment report, identifying the gap between current and desired states

Staff
- Give input on how to measure success
- Give input to assessment strategy
- Write releases and memos

Shared Responsibilities
- Review or complete the Project Management Tool for this phase
- Provide input to vision and mission statements
- Assist in developing assessment instruments and interpreting results
- Support company meetings
- Meet with respective groups to disseminate and collect information
- Provide input to critical success factors for the initiative

responsibilities awaiting them unless the company can release committee members to work on the initiative full time.

How to accomplish this without increasing costs is a particular challenge, especially if the issue facing the company is loss of revenue. However, upper management may have to expend some revenue short-term for long-term gains from the change initiative. There are ways to cover the work of the steering committee members. For example, if everyone else in an affected department or unit temporarily shares a small part of the work, very little increased effort or revenue would be required.

Change Manager

The change manager is responsible for coordinating the activities of the change steering committee. The change manager must establish, monitor, and maintain the schedule by revising and updating the Project Management Tool with the committee members. In addition, the change manager should coordinate and conduct any company meetings that are necessary in order to facilitate smooth work on the change. The change manager should also assist upper management in preparing or revising the corporate vision statement and should assist the change steering committee in developing its mission statement for the change initiative.

Training/Performance Analysts

Training/performance analysts' role is to prepare the change steering committee and company employees for the Assessment phase by explaining, coaching, and/or teaching the various assessment activities listed under Shared Responsibilities (in Table 7.1) and establishing the timetable for each. Many employees are inexperienced with assessment procedures, and coaching can alleviate their fears or misconceptions about their responsibilities. Coaching will also reduce the number of mistakes with the procedures, thus saving time and money.

Training/performance analysts on the change steering committee should lead the effort to develop or purchase any measurement instruments used to collect information during the Assessment phase. They also participate in interpreting the results from the returned assessments once they are analyzed.

Human Resources

Human Resources must actively monitor the Assessment phase to ensure that participants follow company policies and procedures. Human Resources should ensure respect for the privacy of all respondents to any questionnaires or interviews. Additionally, if the organization operates in a union environment, HR will want to ensure it has the union's cooperation.

Staff

Staff members should provide input into the measurement and assessment procedures and instruments. They must be comfortable enough with the process to answer the assessment questions honestly and completely for the groups they represent. The person handling communications should write all memos and other releases about this phase of the change initiative, such as articles for the company newsletter or corporate intranet.

Management Information Services

Technical personnel are charged with assisting in the measurement and analysis of the assessment. If applicable, the selection of a software package with which to analyze the results is important, and this can be the responsibility of the technical members of the change steering committee. Technical personnel should work with the training and performance analysts to begin preparing systems for analysis during the Assessment phase or make decisions to outsource the analysis.

Shared Responsibilities

All change steering committee members must provide inputs to the Assessment phase. They must all support company meetings and participate in writing the mission statement for the change initiative. They should all review the assessment results and provide input and interpretation.

Note: The content of all releases should conform to information agreed on by the steering committee. The steering committee should also agree on an "elevator speech" or "sound bite"—a thirty-second summary about the initiative that all committee members can deliver when asked. Importantly, all change steering committee members should give the same message, so this summary should be in writing, distributed to the committee members, and memorized.

All change steering committee members must assist in completing the Project Management Tool (see Exhibit 6.1) to assign and accept their roles and responsibilities as well as understand all the interdependencies for the Assessment phase.

All steering committee members should also participate in some aspect of the Assessment activities with their respective teams, departments, or divisions. They should determine the assessment activities that must occur in order to gather the data needed. Getting enough of the right information can be critical to the success, in terms of both cost and training outcomes, of your initiative. We list four methods for conducting an assessment in the next section.

The change steering committee should develop a mission statement for the initiative based on and aligned clearly with the vision statement. Here is an example of an internally focused mission statement based on the vision statement presented previously, as developed by a committee charged with finding the most expedient delivery system:

> **Our mission is to find and put in place the best subcontracted system that will make our company number 1 in the delivery of professional moving products.**

The steering committee must also decide, in general terms, the critical success factors that they can use to measure whether or not the change initiative is effective. Examples might be more customers, less down time, fewer complaints, or increased speed to market. Upper management will want to review all of these materials and ensure that they are consistent.

Methodology for Conducting an Assessment

There are four main types of data-gathering methods that require different instruments (Lee & Owens, 2000). You will read about the way that you collect data with each of these methods in Chapter 13 on Gathering Information. Here, our focus is on procedure and strategy. These four types are

1. Self-completion questionnaires;

2. Direct interviews;

3. Focus groups; and

4. Direct observation.

There are ten steps to conducting an assessment:

1. Identify the broad range of goals for the vision: What competencies are needed to successfully achieve the vision? (An excellent book on how to establish competencies for a change initiative is Lucia & Lepsinger, 1999.)

2. Rank the goals in order of importance and show dependencies.

3. Identify the discrepancies between expected and actual performance required to meet a goal. List all the discrepancies as well as missing competencies.

4. Establish priorities for action. Set these against the backdrop of the vision, goals, desired results, and other relevant factors.

5. List the competencies that the organization should develop to achieve the vision.

6. Visit the environment. Look for environmental factors that may impact the issue such as:

   • Noise

   • Speed

- Equipment

- Tools

- Temperature

- Ventilation

7. Create a questionnaire that addresses issues that employees may have in areas such as:

- Management support

- Teamwork

- Empowerment

- Safety

- Job knowledge

Note: Use the appropriate data-collection techniques outlined in Chapter 13 to accomplish the assessment.

---

8. Review all results.

9. Make recommendations.

10. Begin an analysis (this is covered in the next chapter).

 CASE STUDY 1

ASSESSMENT

Having formed its change steering committee, Blumroth entered the Assessment phase. During this phase, Jess led his committee in assisting the organization in exploring how it currently operates and how it desires to operate. The objective for this phase was to conduct an assessment of the organization's needs and to prepare a report with the assessment results.

Jess opened the first change steering committee meeting in this phase by updating the Project Management Tool with everyone. He also announced that he had worked with Joy and that the committee had an initial budget of $50,000 at the outset of this phase. Depending on the decision that the committee made for the type of assessment it would conduct, Jess was certain that he could justify and obtain additional funding.

While there were many assessment options open to the steering committee, the members reached a decision in only one meeting to use paper-and-pencil questionnaires. While the committee debated the viability of online surveys that the company could tabulate electronically, the prevailing feeling was that too many users would feel intimidated by such a process and that the response rate would be higher if employees could just open an envelope containing a survey, complete it, and return it in another envelope. In addition, a professional service was hired at a highly affordable rate of under $25 per hour to enter the data and provide summary reports. The steering committee also agreed to include space for open-ended comments and reserve a place on the form for respondents to indicate if they would like to be called back in order to be interviewed or to ask further questions.

While employees completed the assessment forms, the senior management of the company demonstrated its commitment to the process by meeting to draft a revised version of the vision and mission statements for the organization. This was a critical element so that the change steering committee could then develop its initiative mission statement in alignment with organizational goals. Among other things, these statements served as the "guiding light" for the change initiative and how it would advance the company. Steve, the training/performance analyst, provided assistance in drafting these statements.

The vision statement was

Blumroth Office Systems will be the number 1 office services corporation in market share and customer satisfaction by 2005.

The mission statement was

Blumroth Office Systems is the business community's provider of choice for business supplies and the methods to use them effectively.

The change initiative mission statement, an important tie-in with the two statements above, was

Employees at Blumroth Office Systems accomplish their job responsibilities in the most efficient and effective way possible.

The steering committee asked each employee of the company to complete one of the assessment forms during regular working hours. Steve was on hand to answer questions that employees had when working on their forms. Supervisors provided the release and relief time for employees to complete the forms, since the average time to complete the assessment was twenty-five minutes.

Jess held one company-wide meeting in this phase for managers only. During this meeting, he stressed the fact that all employees should answer the questionnaires honestly and that they should feel free to ask any questions about the forms to the on-call training/performance analysis committee member. Jess also had support from Human Resources (HR), who pledged to ensure confidentiality of responses for those who desired it.

Separately, prior to the distribution of the assessment forms, Bill Duncan from MIS worked with two of his colleagues to assist in preparing for the measurement and analysis of the assessments. These tasks included working with the outsourced service to decide on methods for computer scoring of the forms, statistical analysis, and automated distribution of results.

The time frame to complete the assessment was projected to be five working days with a 95 percent return rate. However, due to vacations and other unavoidable occurrences, the complete assessment took eight working days with a 93 percent response rate. The committee believed that this level of response was excellent.

Because the statistical databases had been set up in advance to analyze the data, MIS worked with the outsourcing service to enter the data as it arrived and processed all of the data within just three hours. The change steering committee met the following day to review all of the reports that the assessment generated.

The results were that 83 percent of all employees had experienced some difficulty, delay, or irritation during the year fulfilling some aspect of their responsibilities, but that only 42 percent had a desire to change the basic way that they worked at the company. Seventy-nine percent of the employees believed that delays in accessing data and obtaining authorized approvals for purchases cost the organization sales and profits. In response to queries about SAP specifically, only 11 percent of all employees reported that they had family members or friends who worked in an SAP-sponsored organization, and a whopping 68 percent of employees had never heard of SAP. Of the 11 percent who had family or friend ties to the system, 79 percent could not specify differences between work done with and without SAP.

The change steering committee met three different times to discuss the impact of the results, with the final two meetings devoted to discussing some follow-up responses offered by various managers in the company about how their departments worked. For the final meeting, several senior management officers attended to lend support to the committee's final recommendation. While not all participants agreed with every opinion expressed during the meeting, the general consensus was that Blumroth was working with processes and procedures that significantly hurt the business and that, unless it implemented a system-wide change, the organization would not fulfill its desired state as expressed in the vision or mission statements.

CASE STUDY 2
ASSESSMENT

The change steering committee at Northcutt entered the Assessment phase having completed two full meetings. Between those meetings, and before they met again at the outset of the Assessment phase, many of the committee members contacted each other for input. Lynn Davis, the internal OD specialist, presented some additional observations to improve the way the committee members asked direct questions to each other and some options that they could use for responding and refuting what they heard. Cherie felt that the committee was truly beginning to jell and she was excited about the prospects for the work ahead of them.

Cherie reminded the committee that the objective for the Assessment phase was to prepare a report that explained the current situation as well as the situation that the organization intended the change initiative to produce. She began by reviewing the Project Management Tool and ensuring that all change steering committee members agreed with its content for this phase. In order to achieve its objective for the phase, the committee had to ensure that it used a viable tool to gather information efficiently and effectively. She also told everyone that the most important input to this phase would come from senior management, who not only initiated the prospects for change at its special retreat, but also would provide support for the initiative throughout the process. CEO Bruce Franklin was a surprise visitor to the meeting, and he assured the committee members of upper management support for the initiative and urged them to complete the work as efficiently, yet as effectively, as possible. He also said that he had established a "hot line" extension in his office exclusively for the use of the change steering committee members.

Cherie asked the members of upper management to provide the committee with the revised vision statement that reflected where they wanted the company to be in the future. The job of helping upper management with this process, as was noted in the Project Management Tool, belonged to Marv and Hugh. As a training and development professional, Marv had experience with several groups in drafting these statements. Hugh provided a financial as well as upper-management perspective to the process.

The bulk of the meeting focused on choosing the method that the organization would use for assessing the current situation. Cherie turned the meeting over to Marv, who had invited two specialists in measurement and evaluation to discuss the features and benefits of different options. The committee considered many factors, such as potential response rate, projected expenses, possible errors, and user comprehension challenges. While some members had to be "won over," the prevailing view was to proceed with an electronic online tool that all employees, regardless of location, could locate on the corporate intranet, complete questions by "clicking" responses, and hit a "send" button to submit the instrument. Virtually every employee in the company had online access, and when Marv assured the committee that his department would write step-by-step instructions for users, coordinate these with the information technology webmasters for posting, and make themselves available for any troubleshooting issues raised by users, the members reached consensus to move forward with the electronic assessment.

The two measurement and evaluation specialists volunteered to take the vision statement developed by senior management and construct a series of relevant questions for the committee to review. The committee agreed that their offer had merit and authorized them to proceed once they had the drafts.

Upper management took just two meetings to provide drafts of the vision statement. Lynn Davis attended these meetings and continually reminded the participants to look forward and assume that the organization was close to an adopted vision. The vision statement was

Northcutt Health Solutions will have the number 1 or number 2 market share in all product lines for medical, dental, and veterinary customers by 2005.

After the change steering committee received the vision, the members worked together to compose a mission statement. The mission statement was

Northcutt Health Solutions provides the highest quality and greatest value paper supplies for the medical, dental, and veterinary industry.

Upper management also decided to construct an additional mission statement and tie together these two statements:

There is no better way to do the work that Northcutt Health Solutions does than the way that our employees do it!

At its next meeting, the steering committee reviewed these drafts, agreed that they were viable, and sent them on to the measurement and evaluation specialists so that they could begin to create items for the questionnaire relevant to these statements. They also worked on some options by which they would analyze the responses once they were tabulated. The committee members received drafts just two days later, and by the committee's next meeting, Marv and Lois (from MIS) had a prototype demonstration ready for everyone to try. Cherie thought it would be a good idea if each committee member took the questionnaire to time the process, provide reactions to the questions, and suggest possible revisions.

Upon doing so, the committee thought that there were too many items and that the time that would be required for employees to complete the questionnaire was unreasonable. They also had several comments about the instructions and identified some glitches in the online system. Committee members reported particular annoyance at the lengthy time delay for a new screen to appear after they had answered all of the items that appeared on an existing screen. Marv agreed to take all of these back to the specialists for correction.

About six business days later, Bruce sent a company-wide e-mail and voice mail announcing that all employees should complete the questionnaire, and he pointed them toward the instructions for doing so on the corporate intranet. Bruce clearly stated that all managers must provide release time for employees to participate in the assessment during normal working hours. He asked Human Resources professionals to monitor this phase and ensure that no one experienced any work repercussions from participating. Human Resources took the additional step of sending an e-mail out to every supervisor ensuring that every employee was allowed time and relief from other responsibilities to complete an assessment. Bruce also stated that if any employee had difficulty completing the questionnaire, he or she should contact Marv in the training and development department immediately. Within one or two days, Marv did receive input from several employees who needed the instructions and questions translated into Spanish. Marv also took the opportunity to teach some managers what an assessment is all about and the purpose it serves within the context of a change initiative.

The committee was amazed at how smoothly everything went during this phase. Bruce had set a deadline for employees to submit their responses to the questionnaire in five business days. More than 95 percent of all employees took and submitted responses. Since the entire process was automated, the measurement and evaluation specialists were able to process the data and interpret the results in just one business day.

All members of the committee worked on drafts of the report that was the output of the Assessment phase. The results were very interesting and provided significant information about the current status as well as direction for the future. Among other results, they included:

• *High specialization and minimal cross-functional work.* Seventy-two percent of all employees who worked in a particular product line in the company admitted knowing very little about processes in other parts of the company.

- *Little understanding of complete processes.* Eighty-one percent of all employees stated that they understood and mastered their own position requirements very well, but had little understanding of the "big picture" and how their contribution ultimately produced sales.

- *Irritated customers.* Sixty-three percent of salespeople admitted that customers in medical, dental, and veterinary services disliked talking to four different Northcutt employees, one for each of the different product lines.

- *Great interest in maximizing profitability.* Ninety-two percent of all employees stated that they would excitedly participate in changes that affected their jobs if those changes resulted in higher profitability for the company and, ultimately, in higher bonuses and increased compensation.

- *Low risk taking.* Seventy-nine percent of all employees reported that they did not feel comfortable experimenting or taking risks in their jobs and did not believe that their managers were tolerant of mistakes or viewed them as a normal part of doing work.

As a result of the data analysis, the assessment report indicated that the organization currently operated in a way that was highly inefficient, duplicative, insular, territorial, and disconnected. This was sufficient information to explain the wide fluctuations in market share and profits. The desired state was to be number 1 or number 2 in all products, with an organization that was highly integrated, sharing, caring, and team-oriented.

At the final meeting in the Assessment phase, Cherie invited senior management officers to attend and comment about the report. Most of them attended the meeting and commented to some committee members "off-line" how upset they were about the status of the situation.

What Could Go Wrong

The Assessment phase contains several potential hazards. You may encounter problems such as these, followed by potential solutions:

Problem: Employees who insist on obtaining more time past the deadline to provide their responses and who have their supervisors support their requests.

Solution: In order to keep the initiative on target for completion, you will likely want to use the data that you have and move forward. These employees had a reasonable amount of time to complete the questionnaire and provide input, and if they could not do so, the change initiative need not be jeopardized.

Problem: Employees who sabotage the results by deliberately providing false responses.

Solution: This is very difficult, if not impossible to control. You can only hope that your sample size is large enough that the inaccurate data is overwhelmed by the vast majority of input that is legitimate.

Problem: Assessment items that do not specifically link to the vision statement constructed by upper management.

Solution: Training/performance analysts should assess the instrument for face and content validity before the change steering committee distributes it to the organization.

Problem: Employees who want to explain their responses rather than simply placing an "x" in a box.

Solution: You can give them the opportunity to write comments by adding a section for that in the online instrument or in a pen-and-paper instrument. However, the primary data should remain the formatted response to the question, so comments should supplement, not replace, the original requested answers.

Problem: A member of upper management who becomes incensed at the assessment results and wants to do away with confidentiality and anonymity.

Solution: The change manager should convey the dangers of upper management only hearing what they want to hear. Since upward communication in an organization is typically "rosy," upper management should be careful not to punish the messenger.

Problem: Change steering committee members who interpret the assessment results in seemingly irreconcilable ways.

Solution: This is not a problem. The change steering committee should welcome differences in viewpoint and should continue discussing the differences until they can reach consensus.

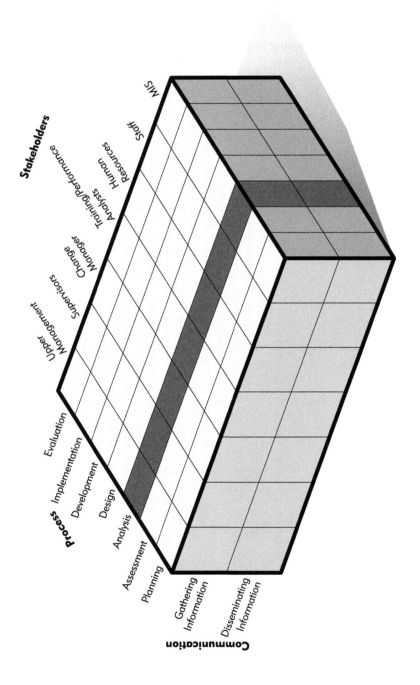

8

Analysis

HAVING COMPLETED AN ASSESSMENT, the next step is to determine how to bridge the gap between the current and the desired situation. This is the phase where the specific change initiative emerges and the change steering committee announces it to the organization. You can choose from a variety of tools to conduct the Analysis phase, which we describe in this chapter.

Inputs

The input to Analysis is a report that fully explains the situation as it exists and what the situation should be in order for the organization to achieve its goals.

Outputs

The output of this phase is a report explaining how to bridge the existing gap.

Responsibilities/Activities

Table 8.1 summarizes stakeholder responsibilities during the Analysis phase.

Upper Management

Upper management must announce the change initiative and approve the budget once the scope is determined at the end of Analysis. The change manager and the staff financial analyst also need to complete the cost/benefit ratio, provide it to upper management for approval, and ensure it is sufficient to justify the change initiative. Upper management must inform the change manager what value the initiative must add to the bottom line. For example, upper management might tell the change manager that the company needs to benefit by $10 million after the first year of implementation of the change. If the financial analyst determines that the project is going to cost $1 million, the cost/benefit ratio is 1:10, meaning that for every dollar spent the company should realize $10 in return. (You can read more about cost/benefit ratio in Chapter 12.)

Supervisors

Supervisors participate in the Analysis phase by coordinating activities with other supervisors, conducting interviews, holding focus groups, sending out and collecting questionnaires, and returning them to the training and performance analysts for data analysis.

Change Manager

The change manager coordinates all meetings, monitors the schedule, and coordinates the completion of the analysis report that contains the change initiative the organization will implement. He or she then presents the report, which includes the cost/benefit analysis, to upper management.

Table 8.1. Responsibilities During Analysis.

Analysis

Upper Management

- Approve the budget for the remainder of the project (Design through Evaluation)
- Approve the cost/benefit analysis ratio
- Announce the specific change initiative

Change Manager

- Coordinate Analysis phase
- Coordinate completing the Project Management Tool for Analysis phase
- Monitor schedule
- Coordinate company meetings
- Present budget to upper management, including cost/benefit information
- Present report to upper management

Human Resources

- Monitor Analysis phase

Management Information Services

- Complete technology analysis

Supervisors

- Coordinate Analysis activities with peers
- Conduct interviews
- Assist in distributing and collecting Analysis surveys

Training/Performance Analyst

- Teach Analysis phase
- Coordinate development of instruments
- Analyze Analysis data
- Write Analysis report

Staff

- Coordinate Analysis activities with peers
- Conduct interviews
- Assist in distributing and collecting Analysis surveys
- Complete cost/benefit analysis
- Write releases and memos

Shared Responsibilities

- Provide inputs to Analysis
- Complete the Project Management Tool for this phase
- Provide input into developing Analysis instruments
- Assist writing releases and memos
- Support company meetings
- Determine methodologies for Evaluation

Training/Performance Analysts

Training and performance analysts must coach and/or provide training on any and all aspects of the Analysis, supervise the construction and validation of the Analysis instruments (such as questionnaires, interview forms, or observation checklists), and analyze returned data.

Human Resources

During this phase, Human Resources does not have any specific responsibilities, but monitors the activities during Analysis and participates in all shared activities.

Staff

Staff members coordinate the Analysis efforts with their peers, conducting interviews, assembling focus groups, distributing and collecting questionnaires, and forwarding them to the training and performance analysts for data analysis. Financial analysts need to assist in completing the cost/benefit analysis. The change steering committee member specializing in communications must continue to write memos and releases about the project.

Management Information Services

MIS steering committee members complete a Technology Analysis using Exhibit 8.5 to determine the specifications or requirements for any new systems required by the change initiative. Systems may be any physical hardware or software, machinery, or other mechanisms. MIS must consider elements such as cost, power, space, range, capacity, form, material, and age. Fitting the best systems to do the job required during this phase will save the company money after implementation.

Shared Responsibilities

Everyone on the change steering committee must participate in the Analysis phase to determine how to bridge the gap identified during the Assessment phase. Each committee member must continue to assist with writing releases and memos to their peers. They must support company meetings, as well as conduct their own meetings to gather analysis data. They must participate in completing the Project Management Tool for Analysis and provide input into suggested methods to evaluate the change.

Note: If you find there is no impact on certain stakeholder groups at the end of the Analysis phase, then those change steering committee members can withdraw from the initiative. However, the groups these committee members represent still would need to be informed of the progress of the change, which can be accomplished through the company newsletter or other releases.

Methodology for Conducting an Analysis

The first step is to select the appropriate type of analysis for the change initiative. In the remainder of this chapter, we describe the procedures you can use to conduct each type of analysis. The analyses to choose from are

1. *Skill Gap*—How prepared are your employees to perform in the new state described by the vision and mission?

2. *Extant Data*—How much do you know, historically, about what other organizations have done when faced with a similar gap?

3. *Environmental*—What are the conditions under which employees perform their jobs?

4. *Issue*—What responsibilities and tasks must be undertaken in order to close the gap?

5. *Critical Incident*—Do you need to prioritize the importance of the responsibilities and tasks to close the gap?

6. *Technology*—Do you need to determine the best tool to use for the organizational infrastructure?

Procedure for Conducting a Skill Gap Analysis

Conduct a Skill Gap Analysis to identify the background and some of the learning characteristics of your target population.

Begin by analyzing the job descriptions that are usually available for positions within a company. These descriptions will either generally or specifically detail the characteristics and types of duties of the affected audience.

Job descriptions usually contain a "catch-all" phrase that will read something like "and other duties as assigned." Be certain to identify whether these other duties fall within or outside of the scope of the issue that is the subject of the change initiative. You can verify generic descriptions and then make modifications, using the data collected during interviews or observations.

The current status of the job description is a critical issue. If the job description was recently revised, it probably accurately reflects the duties of the persons who hold that position. If the job description is not current, you should determine its accuracy by speaking with incumbents, their managers, or other employees who deal with them. The issue of accuracy is one that might well be raised in any case in a time of rapid change and growth in business and industry.

At a minimum, the job descriptions you analyze should contain the following:

1. *Position Title*—The job name. This should be part of an overall organizational structure/hierarchy.

2. *Position Description* (Generic)—A broad description or listing of the actions/activities that are required for successful job performance.

3. *Knowledge, Skills, Attitudes* (KSA)—A specific list of the knowledge, skills, and attitudes required for successful performance.

4. *Proficiency Measures*—A list and explanation of the performance measures used for successful completion.

Note: If job descriptions do not exist for a position, they should be developed during the Assessment phase.

From the job descriptions, make a list of all the competencies that exist among current employees. You will use this information at the end of the Analysis phase to determine what skills exist, who has the skills, and where there are skill gaps.

Use the tool in Exhibit 8.1 to verify that the critical steps/skills and list of interdependencies you have identified accurately reflect their current state and contain the current or projected need. The steering committee members should validate the accuracy of this tool when it is completed.

Exhibit 8.1. Skill Gap Analysis Tool.

Instructions:

1. List each skill from job descriptions.
2. List names of all employees who have that skill.
3. List the skill level based on the definitions at the bottom of the tool.
4. Determine whether or not the skill will be required after the change.
5. Identify new skills that the organization will require after the change that are currently not in job descriptions.
6. Determine whether any employees in the company have those skills through interviews and skills inventories.
7. Determine the level of the new skill employees have.
8. Use the comments sections for notes regarding skills issues (for example, "need expert level, highest level is novice. Can train employees to assume new jobs.")

Project:			
Vision Statement:			
Mission Statement:			
Skill	**Employee Names**	**Level of Skill**	**Skill Required After the Change**
		☐ Expert ☐ Proficient ☐ Novice	☐ Yes ☐ No
		☐ Expert ☐ Proficient ☐ Novice	☐ Yes ☐ No
		☐ Expert ☐ Proficient ☐ Novice	☐ Yes ☐ No
		☐ Expert ☐ Proficient ☐ Novice	☐ Yes ☐ No
		☐ Expert ☐ Proficient ☐ Novice	☐ Yes ☐ No
		☐ Expert ☐ Proficient ☐ Novice	☐ Yes ☐ No

(Continued)

Exhibit 8.1. Skill Gap Analysis Tool. (*Continued*)

New Skills Required by the Change	Employee Names	Level of Skill	Comments
		☐ Expert ☐ Proficient ☐ Novice	
		☐ Expert ☐ Proficient ☐ Novice	
		☐ Expert ☐ Proficient ☐ Novice	
		☐ Expert ☐ Proficient ☐ Novice	

Novice   entry level—would require extensive training and time to develop required level of skill

Proficient adequate skill to perform the task

Expert   high degree of ability to perform the skill—could lead and train others who perform the skill

Procedure for Conducting an Extant Data Analysis

Extant Data Analysis (which might be called benchmarking) searches for what information already exists within or outside of the company for purposes of implementing the vision. Examining past successful or unsuccessful efforts to achieve a desired state similar to the one your organization is undertaking can be very useful in speeding up the implementation of your initiative, as you can learn from past successes and mistakes.

A search for what your company or other companies have done in the past regarding the subject of a new desired state outlined in the vision once may have been a rather daunting task, but with advances in telecommunications and computer technology, this search has become relatively simple to complete. The Extant Data Analysis provides an added level of confidence and reliability for those who take the time to complete it.

There are many sources for this extant data—from other companies, to advertisements, to vendors and consultants at professional conferences. The World Wide Web is an excellent source of information. Many public or corporate libraries offer online computer searches of information on nearly any topic. Information searches can be conducted using bulletin board services (BBS) and special interest groups or list-servs on the Internet. Some of the best organizations for online searches are the Corporate Leadership Council (www.corporateleadershipcouncil.com), Corporate University Exchange (www.corpu.com), Society for Human Resource Management (www.SHRM.org), American Society for Training and Development (www.astd.org), and Organizational Development Network (www.odnetwork. org). Search costs vary from free to a fixed fee per search to a charge per unit of search time and amount of information generated.

The key to successful Extant Data Analysis searches all comes down to organization. When developing questions for a computer search, write your question or questions on the topic as narrowly as the issue can be defined. The computer searches on key words and can only give back information based on what you input.

Extant Data Analyses also include the examination and evaluation of the suitability and possible use of existing solutions that you find. There is no need to reinvent the wheel if the solution already exists through a means that you can purchase and adapt to meet your particular need. Someone still has to *read* the information generated from the computer search. Or someone has to find the information if the search provides only a bibliography. Sometimes the time available for this review is limited, so reducing the amount of material that you have to search for and collect requires you to select the most relevant data in the fastest way possible.

Your analysis should progress through the following steps:

1. Determine what it is that you are looking for. Is it information on an entire solution, or on one or more parts?

2. Identify likely sources:

   • Internal resources

   • Professional organizations

   • Training vendors

- Universities/schools

- Libraries

- Other commercial search facilities

3. Gather information.

4. Determine the usability of the information you have selected. Match information for critical analysis, version availability, amount of extraneous information, potential for modification to your needs, and cost of "build versus buy." You also need to consider the timeliness of the information that you might find. Use the form in Exhibit 8.2 to record your notes.

5. Make a decision to "buy" a solution or hire a consultant if the results of your analysis determine it would not be possible to produce the solution internally within your timeline and budget.

6. Make a decision to "build" the solution if the results of your analysis do not locate a usable or adaptable solution.

Exhibit 8.2. Extant Data Analysis Form.

1. Source of Information:

2. Type of Information:

Article _____

Book _____

Course Material _____

User Manual _____

Vendor _____

Other _____

3. Summary of Information Found:

4. Probability of Use:

Very Low	Low	Moderate	High	Very High
1	2	3	4	5

Procedure for Conducting an Environmental Analysis

If you actually observed a problem or issue during the Assessment phase, you may have noted the physical conditions in which employees perform a job. If you did not make this observation, taking the time to conduct an Environmental Analysis can help you zoom in on the environmental factors that impact performance. There are both positive and adverse impacts or issues that enable or prevent employees from doing their jobs. The areas of impact include:

- *Management Support*—Do those in authority encourage and stand behind the employees and let them do their jobs?

- *Teamwork*—Is there inter- and intra-departmental cooperation that enables work to be done in a timely manner?

- *Empowerment*—Are employees permitted to make decisions without consulting management when it comes to the responsibilities of their own work?

- *Safety*—Is the physical environment, including lighting, ergonomics, and workplace layout, a safe place to work where employees can do their jobs without fear of injury?

- *Job Knowledge*—Do employees have the skills and knowledge to complete their jobs?

Visiting the workplace is the best way to conduct an Environmental Analysis. Any solution you develop will be designed to ensure successful change for the current state of affairs. Before you can be sure about what to change, you need to examine the environment for factors that allow successful performance.

Viewing videotapes of the environment will provide some data, but will not allow you to question performers "real time" or experience some of the environmental factors that affect performance. Also, with video, you can only see what the lens of the camera sees, causing you to miss practically everything on the periphery.

Your next step is to confirm your observations and gather supporting information. An effective method is to develop a brief questionnaire based on your observations and any related environmental issues that employees may experience and then use this questionnaire to interview the employees who perform the job.

You can refer to the questionnaire and interview guidelines discussed in Chapter 13 on Gathering Information. However, we believe that making observations is the best method to collect data. See the environment yourself, first-hand.

Procedure for Conducting an Issue Analysis

Issue Analysis is an outgrowth of Environmental Analysis; it requires you to determine the characteristics of the issue that the organization's vision focuses on, then define the elements that comprise each responsibility that the vision requires. Within every element are subelements, or steps, necessary to fulfill the issue.

A well-structured Issue Analysis should result in a list of all the tasks required to achieve the vision and for a successful change initiative. When conducting an Issue Analysis, you need to identify and define each of the following:

1. *Project*—A name for the vision, for example: Integrating Production and Shipping Processes.

2. *Issue*—Major areas of responsibilities that individuals perform. You usually state issues as a general area of responsibility, with action words ending in "ing," for example: Aligning production and shipping processes.

3. *Element*—A specific function or meaningful unit within the issue, for example: Handoff of machine parts between production and shipping.

4. *Sub-elements*—A step, action, operation, or activity that is a logical segment of an element that advances the work, for example: Production stores parts in warehouse but does not notify shipping.

Exhibit 8.3 provides a worksheet you can use to record each issue and its related elements and sub-elements.

Note: Rejecting an area of responsibility at the Issue level automatically rejects all elements and sub-elements. Critical and non-critical issues may still have elements and sub-elements that you can reject.

Exhibit 8.3. Issue Analysis Form.

Project Name:	Complete as part of Critical Incident Analysis	Complete after you write objectives
Issue 1 _____ _____	☐ Critical ☐ Non-critical ☐ Reject	**Number** _____ Objective
Element 1.1 _____ _____	☐ Critical ☐ Non-critical ☐ Reject	_____ Objective
Sub-element 1.1.1 _____ _____	☐ Critical ☐ Non-critical ☐ Reject	_____ Objective
Sub-element 1.1.2 _____ _____	☐ Critical ☐ Non-critical ☐ Reject	_____ Objective
Element 1.2 _____ _____	☐ Critical ☐ Non-critical ☐ Reject	_____ Objective
Sub-element 1.2.1 _____ _____	☐ Critical ☐ Non-critical ☐ Reject	_____ Objective
Sub-element 1.2.2 _____ _____	☐ Critical ☐ Non-critical ☐ Reject	_____ Objective
Issue 2 _____ _____	☐ Critical ☐ Non-critical ☐ Reject	_____ Objective
Element 2.1 _____ _____	☐ Critical ☐ Non-critical ☐ Reject	_____ Objective
Sub-element 2.1.1 _____ _____	☐ Critical ☐ Non-critical ☐ Reject	_____ Objective
Sub-element 2.1.2 _____ _____	☐ Critical ☐ Non-critical ☐ Reject	_____ Objective

Critical must be addressed
Non-critical can be addressed, time and budget permitting
Reject not relevant to the issue

Procedure for Conducting a Critical Incident Analysis

We have placed Issue Analysis before Critical Incident Analysis to help focus separately each of these tasks. To clarify, the focus of Issue Analysis is on ascertaining all the related elements of the issue at hand. The focus of Critical Incident Analysis is on prioritizing and selecting those tasks that will be included in the initiative. However, you cannot do a Critical Incident Analysis without first having completed an Issue Analysis. The following steps and instructions illustrate the integration of the two analyses:

1. Determine the issues from Issue Analysis that are critical and that you must address.

2. Identify the issues that are non-critical but that you can address, time and budget permitting.

3. Determine those issues that you will reject because they do not impact the change initiative.

You will use the Issue Analysis Form (Exhibit 8.3) to complete these steps.

Those issues and elements that employees perform well on the job need to be a part of the analysis in order to determine how employees complete them. There may be a need to train others in the same procedures. Identifying those issues and elements in an organization that employees perform well and then replicating them is known as Appreciative Inquiry (Watkins & Mohr, 2001).

Some of the primary reasons for rejecting an issue for inclusion in a change are

- Element is *seldom* evident;

- Element is *not critical*; or

- Element is *easily learned without formal intervention*.

Critical issues are those that employees must complete in order to successfully make the change. Rate each issue identified during Issue Analysis on the Critical Incident form as follows. You may want to consider the following when you establish your norms:

- How often the issues arises—more often generally indicates more critical;

- The severity of the consequences for failure to address the issue; and
- Any special skills inherent in the issue required to make the change.

Using your established measures of criticality, you should then:

1. Review each issue with a subject-matter expert (SME) or exemplary performer;

2. Validate the critical aspects of each issue;

3. Validate the elements that must be included;

4. Create a hierarchy of issues; and

5. List all issues that are interdependent.

Use focus groups, observations, direct interviews, and questionnaires (or any combinations that you feel are necessary) to determine the critical incidents. Whichever technique(s) you use, the basic procedure is to review the issues that participants generated during the Issue Analysis. Exhibit 8.4 can be used to evaluate each issue.

Transfer the final decision to the Issue Analysis Form—Column 2 (Exhibit 8.3).

Note: There is no "master key" to the rating scales listed above. There is no mathematical average, benchmarked norm, or other formula that will provide you with a totally sound basis for making a decision. To have each member of a project team rate the components independently does not yield an accurate average, as each team member rates the component from his or her own perspective. Use a group consensus to arrive at the rating. Use the rating scales above and the priority levels in Exhibit 8.3 to make decisions based on customer needs and professional judgment.

Procedure for Conducting a Technology Analysis

A Technology Analysis (Lee & Owens, 2000) will identify the technological infrastructure that will be required to support any solution called for by the vision. You should identify the current infrastructure availability, the capability or reliability of each component, and who in the affected parts of the

Exhibit 8.4. Issue Rating Form.

Instructions: Rate each issue in the categories below:

Issue: _____

1. **Frequency**—How often will the issue be evident?

Never		Sometimes		Always
1	2	3	4	5

2. **Number of Employees Affected**—What percentage of the target population will be impacted?

Few		Some		Many
0–10%	11–30%	31–70%	71–90%	91–100%

3. **Difficulty**—How difficult is it to address this issue?

Very Easy	Easy	Difficult	Very Difficult	Impossible
1	2	3	4	5

4. **Criticality**—How important is it for the success of the change?

Not Critical	Important	Critical
N	I	C

5. **Time**—How long should it take to resolve this issue?

Less than 10 Minutes	10–20 Minutes	20–30 Minutes	30–40 Minutes	40–50 Minutes
0	1	2	3	4
50–60 Minutes	More than One Hour	More than 3 Hours	More than 6 Hours	More than One Day
5	6	7	8	9

6. **Impact**—What is the probability that this issue will affect the change?

Very Low	Low	Moderate	High	Very High
1	2	3	4	5

7. **Delay**—At what point in the change will the issue arise?

Two Weeks	One Month	Three Months	Six Months	One Year
1	2	3	4	5

8. **Interdependencies**—Are the various issues interconnected?

Hardly	Somewhat	Moderately	Very	Extremely
1	2	3	4	5

organization has access to each technology. The Technology Assessment Tool in Exhibit 8.5 lists six types of infrastructure to examine. Use this tool to complete your Technology Analysis.

Analysis Report

The data from all of the analyses comprise the Analysis Report. This report announces the change initiative that the organization should undertake to make the vision statement a reality. The change manager will compile all of

Exhibit 8.5. Technology Analysis Tool.

1. List the types of technology available. For example, if employees have access to e-mail, put a check mark in the "Availability" column of the tool next to "e-mail."
2. Document the capability strength of each technology. For example, if e-mail is stretched to capacity, circle Low. If e-mail has potential to be used after the change is implemented, circle High.
3. Document the number and percentage of employees who have access to the technology.

This tool provides you the information necessary to assist in making decisions about purchasing or implementing particular types of technology for a change initiative. If a particular tool is unavailable, but has great capability, you may consider purchasing and implementing it. If a tool is available, but low in capability, you may consider replacing it with another option.

Technology Use	Examples of Technology Use	Availability	Capability	Access (percent)
Communication	Phone conferencing		Low Med High	
	E-mail		Low Med High	
	Chat rooms		Low Med High	
	Newsgroups		Low Med High	
	List servers		Low Med High	
Reference materials, online help	Web sites		Low Med High	
	Work process and procedures		Low Med High	
	Databases		Low Med High	
	Phone lists		Low Med High	
	Course catalogues		Low Med High	
	Scheduling and appointments		Low Med High	
	Course notes		Low Med High	
	Instructor's notes		Low Med High	
	Abstracts		Low Med High	
	Technical manuals		Low Med High	
	Videos		Low Med High	
	Graphics and photos		Low Med High	
Testing and assessment: online testing, tracking, reporting	Electronic self-assessment databases		Low Med High	
	Electronic tracking databases		Low Med High	
	Electronic reporting databases		Low Med High	
	Security (access, authentication, confidentiality)		Low Med High	

(Continued)

Exhibit 8.5. Technology Analysis Tool. (*Continued*)

Technology Use	Examples of Technology Use	Availability	Capability	Access (percent)
Distribution: sending throughout the organization	CD-ROM		Low Med High	
	Diskette		Low Med High	
	Video		Low Med High	
	Audio		Low Med High	
	Downloading		Low Med High	
Delivery: receiving throughout the organization	Dedicated audio and video servers		Low Med High	
	Multimedia computers		Low Med High	
	Video teleconferencing		Low Med High	
Design and development expertise: infrastructure design, development, maintenance, resources (include anticipated upgrades)	Video production		Low Med High	
	Audio production		Low Med High	
	Graphics production		Low Med High	
	Online help and reference system production		Low Med High	
	CBT authoring		Low Med High	
	Web authoring		Low Med High	
	Testing database		Low Med High	
	Statistical program		Low Med High	

the forms into one document. The staff communication specialist can assist in writing the executive summary. The change manager must also work with the financial analyst to deliver the budget for the project. The budget would include the cost/benefit analysis covered in Chapter 12. Upper management must approve the report, the budget, and the cost/benefit ratio before the initiative can move forward.

CASE STUDY 1
ANALYSIS

The Assessment report substantiated the presence of a gap between the current and desired state for Blumroth. But exactly what change would the steering committee recommend? Not only would the committee need to consider options for bridging the gap, but they had to find out the barriers, obstacles, paths, methods, and options that they needed to be aware of.

Jess reviewed the Project Management Tool with the change steering committee and updated several items. From that update, different members of the change steering committee spent the major amount of their time in this stage conducting the appropriate analyses. In some aspects of the analysis, the committee members enlisted the assistance of their direct reports and peers. All analysis tools were employed in the analysis.

After several meetings to revise drafts, senior management was satisfied with the revised mission and vision statements. Under the CEO's signature, every department manager received an individual letter requesting him or her to read the mission and vision statements to employees. A representative from the committee attended as many of these meetings as possible to answer any questions. After everyone had the opportunity to understand the direction and the rationale, they were much more satisfied.

The MIS analysis teams provided the results and interpretation from the assessment to all supervisors in the organization. Through a memo, senior management encouraged each supervisor to share the results with all of their employees. They also asked the supervisors to obtain a general validation of the results by asking their employees: "Is this right?" "Does this apply here?" or "How much of a problem is this?" More than 85 percent of all supervisors provided some positive validation back to senior management.

Recall that the Assessment results indicated that very few users had even heard of SAP, the system that was first introduced, yet not pushed, by Frank Adams, the CEO. Even those who had knowledge of the system would not be aware of the specific system issues that were necessary to implement SAP, or any other similar solution, at Blumroth. Hence, Jess endorsed the decision that every employee in the company should participate in the process-mapping sessions that described the way that he or she performed certain tasks and functions in the organization. Regardless of the specific solution that Blumroth would eventually implement, process mapping is a requisite activity. He reasoned that without widespread involvement and participation in the way that Blumroth implemented a system, there would be very little buy-in to the change and very poor results.

Jess, Steven Barry, and several training/performance analysis professionals met to construct a brief questionnaire to send to each user's manager. This instrument attempted to identify the skill levels that each of the users possessed in process description methods, such as flow charting, linear thinking, and information mapping. While very few employees had even heard of these terms, the purpose of the assessment was to determine the skills and aptitude that served as the foundation for using these processes. In addition, several items on the questionnaire focused on worker style and preference issues. These included questions such as "Do you work better as a participant in a group or one-on-one?" and "Do you learn better from visual stimuli or from reading text?"

The ultimate goal was that each department would produce fully detailed, visual, linear process maps of each of the functions that its employees performed on the job. These maps are step-by-step delineations of how a department completes a process. Employees initially gather as a unit to draw out the maps on flip-chart paper and later transfer them to a software program, such as Visio®. Examples of processes include (1) how an employee checks out a book from the company library, (2) how Human Resources places an employee on FMLA (Family and Medical Leave Act), and (3) how the MIS department prioritizes help desk requests.

The departments were to submit the maps describing the way that they actually performed the function, not the way they wished they could perform it or the way that others wished they could perform it. Once all the processes were mapped out, they could be entered into a system, which would then identify redundancies, inefficiencies, roadblocks, barriers, and other issues that could hinder organizational effectiveness. Correcting these problems was to be the ultimate result of the change initiative and would allow the organization to realize its vision and mission. One reason that SAP was a leading favorite as a solution was that it comes with standard procedures, and MIS could enter some of the company's processes fairly quickly by modifying variables, codes, or other formatting items.

The Extant Data Analysis revealed that many high-quality sources on process mapping functions were available. These included self-instruction manuals, online tutorials, and CD-ROM/multimedia courses, as well as public seminars taught by consulting companies. In addition, several managers had experimented with process mapping for informal decision making during their departmental meetings over the years. The change steering committee decided early in this process that, since the goal was to involve as many employees in the construction of these maps as possible, the committee would not limit the training to any single source or method.

Each manager could decide who received training and how he or she would obtain that training. The company allocated $250,000 for the training.

A Skill Gap Analysis revealed severe constraints in both training for and implementing the mapping sessions. While change steering committee members were not able to visit with each of the managers in every department where the employees would provide maps of the processes, a sample of those departments revealed a host of problems. Recall that the Assessment results indicated that, while most users experienced problems of redundancy and inefficiency, less than half wanted to do anything to change the situation. Hence, motivating employees to initiate, let alone complete, the process mapping for each of the functions they performed was a major issue for the committee. This problem was delegated to the supervisors and staff members who served on the change steering committee to address and solve. Further, the analysis indicated that, with the exception of MIS employees, most departments did not have employees who had ever visually depicted a work process, and those who had experienced doing so had not mapped to the level of detail required by this initiative. In addition, only a few employees worked in closed offices, where training could be conducted without disturbing others and where the user could concentrate completely on how to participate in a mapping session. A vast majority of the users worked in open, cubicle-type arrangements. Some of these were in high-traffic, high-noise areas where on-the-job training would be most difficult to conduct.

The Issue Analysis was lengthy and involved. The significant results were that employees had to become familiar with obtaining and interpreting all types of data in many different ways. This represented a significant cultural shift in the way the organization did business, rather than simply a change in job function. The basic ways that many employees performed their jobs would change drastically as a result of implementing the desired vision. Not only did this mean that employees would access data in a different way, but also that they could expect a fundamental shift in the basic responsibilities defined in their jobs. Therefore, each employee had to master new functions in order to achieve the job objective or outcomes that he or she was responsible for producing. The major functions included accessing sales volume and profit data, inventory data, employee data, customer data, supplier data, and vendor data and interpreting and reporting information from the data in different ways, using word processing, spreadsheets, graphics, statistical analyses, electronic mail, and databases. Whereas in the past the company may have had entire departments devoted to building a PowerPoint® presentation from statistical data, with the advent of a shared data system (of which SAP is one), most users now were charged with the responsibility of doing these reports themselves.

Critical Incident Analysis determined that the most beneficial aspects to focus on were the way employees accessed and maneuvered through the system, handled security issues, obtained help as necessary, and transferred the information coherently to a report or final product. The security issues were handled primarily by creating profiles that gave users access to data and system functions. Although employees had different job titles and different roles, creating profiles allowed multiple users similar access to data. Conversations with users of shared data systems in other organizations revealed that these tasks were the most often performed and incurred the most serious consequences if done incorrectly.

From all of these analyses, the change steering committee would be able to write the objectives during the Design phase and tailor the content appropriately.

The bottom line for this phase was the report that the committee unanimously recommended a change for full-scale implementation of SAP at Blumroth within eighteen months. The committee reached this decision after conducting the analyses described in this phase, researching the capabilities of SAP and other options, meeting with representatives from other companies that had implemented SAP, and investigating budget constraints for all phases of the company's operations. The committee's recommendation was accepted by the entire senior management team of the organization, and word immediately spread throughout the company that a change in fundamental processes was imminent. Remember that the outcome of Analysis is a plan for bridging the gap, not the design for how the organization will implement the plan, which is in the next phase.

Many other activities took place during the Analysis phase. Let's look at some of them, especially what happened as soon as the content of the Analysis report became well-known.

At Blumroth, the impact of the proposed solution was almost immediate. Rumors, suspicion, and doubts ran rampant throughout the company. A great number of employees expressed resistance to changing to SAP as, predictably, they were very comfortable doing their jobs the way they had been doing them for many years. While training/performance analysts and staff and supervisor members of the committee reassured employees that they would receive help in getting "up-to-speed" on the new system, confusion still reigned supreme.

Jess Albertson was quite busy in this phase as well. He found himself clarifying misconceptions and resolving conflicts throughout the organization. For instance, two division managers (from accounting systems and marketing support) equally believed that their employees should have the first training and first access to the system. One manager spread the absurd rumor that the company would provide laptops for employees to take home if they agreed to check data at least twice during a weekend. Lynn Shaunessey from MIS presented Jess with a letter signed by all of her employees that protested the purchase of licensing for SAP in favor of using this money for increased compensation.

When Joy and a group of her peers had completed the cost/benefit ratio, she presented it to the change steering committee. The figures revealed a striking financial benefit to the organization by implementing SAP. The analysis revealed that in a five-year period, the company would gain more than five times in profits what it spent for the system.

Two teams from MIS were busy analyzing the specifications for accommodating SAP on the company servers and systems. For example, each personal computer in the company was investigated for its suitability to run and install the necessary programs. Some computers needed additional RAM (random access memory), others required more gigahertz for speed, while others required more space on the hard disk. Note that this upgrade exhibits a true investment in the future. MIS professionals were very excited about creating employee goodwill by providing them faster computers to do their jobs, which had to happen to use SAP.

MIS divided employees who had computers on their desks into three classes: those whose hardware was adequate and only needed to install the software to run SAP, those whose computers could simply be upgraded with more memory or incidental equipment before installing the systems, and those who needed completely new hardware and software. From the priority list established in the previous phase, MIS worked with the change steering committee to determine in which order the various departments would receive and install the equipment and software. Money did not exist in the budget for every department and every user to receive the upgraded hardware and software at once; therefore, constructing a priority list was critical.

MIS also identified numerous barriers that might cause SAP to fail for some users. These problems included not having enough memory to run the software to access portions of SAP. The concern was felt less in the corporate office and more in the field and remote locations, such as stores, where users typically accessed programs on a laptop computer with a 28K or 56K modem. The downside was that the response time for the system with these two speeds was very low. When a person in the field needed to access or refresh a data slice, he or she found it very time-consuming, if not inconvenient, to do so. It was one thing to download a file in the comfort of a hotel room; it was entirely another thing to do so at an airport gate, in a client's waiting room, or in a restaurant. As a result, MIS immediately set about to overcome these barriers by checking the hardware configurations of all company computers, including those operated by employees outside of the corporate office.

Clearly, the change steering committee left the Analysis phase with quite a job ahead of them. Unless the various departments and divisions did well with their process mapping, and unless the right programs were available on the right computers for the right users, and unless employees who expressed fears or reservations about the change were placated, the chances for success with the change initiative were minimal.

CASE STUDY 2
ANALYSIS

The Assessment report provided the gap between current and desired states for Northcutt Health Solutions. What was not clear entering the Analysis phase was exactly how the change would take place. Precisely what would the organization do? What were the options and, more importantly, what were the potential "rocks in the road"? The task of the committee in this phase was to formulate a plan to bridge the gap and identify each of the barriers, obstacles, paths, and methods for each option that they needed to be aware of in order to proceed correctly. Ever since the executive staff meeting had ended, everyone knew the organization would change in some way. The question was simply "how?"

Cherie stated that, in the best interest of maintaining accurate and updated communication, she would urge Bruce to hold another company-wide meeting in the very near future. At that meeting, she wanted him to outline the general direc-tion the change would take, discuss the next steps, and answer as many questions as possible from the group of employees who attended.

At the outset of this phase, having been thoroughly prepped by Hugh from a financial perspective, Cherie sought and received approval from senior manage-ment for the budget for the remainder of the project, along with the return-on-investment projections. The report projected a modest 5 percent return in the first year due to the many employees working through "learning curves," but projected a 33 percent return by the third year and a 62 percent return in the fifth year as the company fully realized its potential for increased efficiencies.

At the first meeting in this phase, Cherie asked Marv to provide an overview of all of the various activities and tools that the committee members could make use of during this phase. The committee also reviewed the Project Management Tool for the phase and made numerous updates to the notes they had completed earlier.

Remember that, while the committee was aware of the option that the organi-zation would consolidate and restructure in order to achieve its vision, it was any-one's guess as to how and to what extent that would happen.

Lynn Davis and some other HR professionals provided various managers across the four product lines in the company with a questionnaire to identify the key skills required in their jobs and to rate the knowledge and skill levels that their employees possessed in the projected "new" jobs performed by others. These questionnaires identified the major deficiencies that the company had perpetuated by running itself in silos and documented that very few employees knew, or even were aware of, processes outside of their own specific responsibilities.

As the discussion ensued, some members of the change steering committee expressed concern that cross-functional training designed to broaden knowledge and skill across various levels of the organization would produce more "shortcuts" and "how to get by" training than a focus on doing a job optimally. For this reason, all of the members endorsed a thorough Issue Analysis for the major outcomes that each employee was responsible for producing. From this analysis, the training/performance analysts could clearly identify which skills were high-priority and then provide or design materials to facilitate proper cross-functional training. While certain members objected to the more than six weeks that would be required to complete such an Issue Analysis, everyone agreed that it would take more time to fix a solution that was not done right the first time than it would to allocate the resources and complete it properly. As a result of the meeting, and due to the fact that Northcutt's employees were technology-savvy, Marv initiated an Issue Analysis from training and performance, and Lois initiated a technology Issue Analysis with the help of other MIS professionals.

Since the change steering committee was committed to running a pilot for the change initiative, it became obvious to Cherie and Bruce that Human Resources would need to be the first department to transform from a "silo-specific" department to a consolidated one. The review of the complete Project Management Tool revealed that, for many employee issues throughout the phases, HR would be a driving force. As a result, the team greatly accelerated many of the decisions about which HR employees would stay with the company in the consolidated function and exactly how to align their roles and functions.

As a result of performing these analyses, the change steering committee would be able to write the objectives during the Design phase and align the content appropriately. During this phase, the committee also continued its company-wide communication efforts.

A team of MIS professionals completed the Technology Analysis and determined that the vast majority of employees had both capability and availability for online means of communicating and transferring information. In addition, based on the reduced number of help-desk telephone calls and e-mails, many salespeople who worked outside of the corporate office had become more acclimated to the computer-oriented way to do their jobs.

Bruce and Cherie decided to insert new energy into the company by posting and sharing all of the revised vision statements and allowing full access to the processes and procedures undertaken by the change steering committee. The second company-wide meeting included a segment where Bruce proclaimed that the change initiative would be open to full scrutiny from any interested employees and that all questions were welcome and would receive answers. He further stated that if a member of the change steering committee could not answer a question, it would only be under the condition that a member did not know, rather than would not share, information. This open-door announcement raised the trust and, ultimately, the productivity of many employees.

The final report from the Analysis phase specified all of the tools, systems, knowledge, and skills that would be necessary to accomplish the proposed reorganization, along with a plan for accomplishing it. The plan had to balance the time managers and employees would spend learning tasks for their "new" jobs and completing the requirements for their existing jobs. The report also specified the massive amounts of technological adjustments that the computer systems would need to incorporate in order to consolidate departments that were previously in "silos" into one centralized operation. Finally, the report indicated a proposed method for aligning customers with salespeople in order to ensure proper coverage and growth of the business.

Human Resources professionals participated in an initial examination of the impact of the change initiative on jobs. The focus of their analysis was not so much on the content or nature of the jobs, but on the number of people who would be required to perform the work. The results indicated that the company would not need nearly the number of employees under the consolidated functions and, therefore, would need a system by which to identify which employees would remain with the company, along with a process by which employees could interview for other positions. In addition, Human Resources professionals began to consider transition options for employees, including transfers, training, and severance.

Given the vision statement and the assessment results, the steering committee and upper management agreed that the company was not organized in the most efficient manner to conduct its business. They agreed that the organization of the company was the single biggest factor producing the unsatisfactory results in market share and profits. They also agreed that, unless the company vigorously reorganized, it would not improve its situation in either factor. Particularly troubling to everyone was the revelation that separate departments in each product line that served the same basic function or service (sales, marketing, finance and accounting, Human Resources) shared little or no information, and basically each seemed to "invent" and "reinvent" the wheel. A cost analysis estimate from the financial directors of the time and resources wasted by this alignment produced staggering figures that clearly were a drain on the company's bottom line. In addition, the team was upset that the alignment of its salesforce required employees to "pass each other on the highway," in that up to four different people would call on the same customer, each representing a different facet of the company. One participant from

upper management was so upset at the estimate of money wasted by this procedure that she actually walked out of the meeting to compose herself.

Two highly visible outcomes were agreed on. First, the organization would cen-
tralize its marketing department, finance and accounting operations, and Human
Resources department at the Kansas City corporate headquarters, thus dissolving
the separate silos for each product line. The second was that the salesforce would
be realigned by territory, with each salesperson in a geographic area representing
all of the company's products and services, thus providing each customer a single
face from Northcutt.

Some employees at all levels and from all departments expressed concerns
about the proposed changes. Rumors about job security resurfaced, and several
employees even expressed their lack of desire to learn new skills, obtain new knowledge, or work with new people. Predictably, most employees were resistant to the
change simply because they were very comfortable doing their jobs the way they
had been performing them for many years. Although internal communications such
as e-mails, voice mails, and the change initiative posting on the corporate intranet
reassured employees that they would be treated fairly and trained properly, the company still had an air of anxiety as employees went through their daily routines. In
addition, there seemed to be a lack of energy and productivity.

The change steering committee left the Analysis phase with some apprehension
about the quality of training that its managers and employees would need to execute in order to accommodate the change in the nature of jobs within the organization. While specific details were still unclear, all members expressed confidence
that they had accurately identified the jobs as well as the required capabilities quite
well. They also believed that the decision to allow existing managers and employees to cross-train others would work, given the existence of the job requirements as
identified by the Issue Analysis.

Overall, the report from the Analysis phase called for a realignment along
customer groups from product groups, along with the consolidation of what were
previously product-specific support departments into corporate headquarters. The
report indicated the affected groups, which were Sales, Marketing, Finance,
Accounting, and Human Resources.

The change steering committee provided the report to upper management and
prepared itself for the Design phase.

What Could Go Wrong

In the Analysis phase, you may run into various obstacles for which you must be prepared:

Problem: The initiative gets behind the projected schedule due to a backlog in interpreting some of the analyses.

Solution: You may want to consider enlisting some external support to reduce the backlog. The challenge is to ensure that the people hired to assist with the interpretation are knowledgeable and qualified with the specific problem at hand. In many cases, you may save money simply by adjusting the timetable and relying on internal sources.

Problem: Upper management provides a cost/benefit ratio that change steering committee members believe is unrealistic.

Solution: The change manager and staff financial analyst should meet with members of upper management and listen to the reasons that they believe the cost/benefit ratio is justified. If that meeting is unfulfilling, the change manager and staff financial analyst should present an alternative case and attempt to convince upper management of the viability of their reasoning.

Problem: Employees complete the Technology Analysis Tool to measure what they want, rather than what they have.

Solution: Staff members from MIS who work on or with the change steering committee should be able to recognize the equipment, systems, and capabilities that each department or division in the organization currently possesses and then either dismiss the data or, if time permits, ask the user to resubmit the Technology Analysis Tool.

Problem: The technology analysts might indicate a delivery system that the company's infrastructure will not support.

Solution: The change steering committee has to complete a persuasive business case to justify the cost to purchase the additional system.

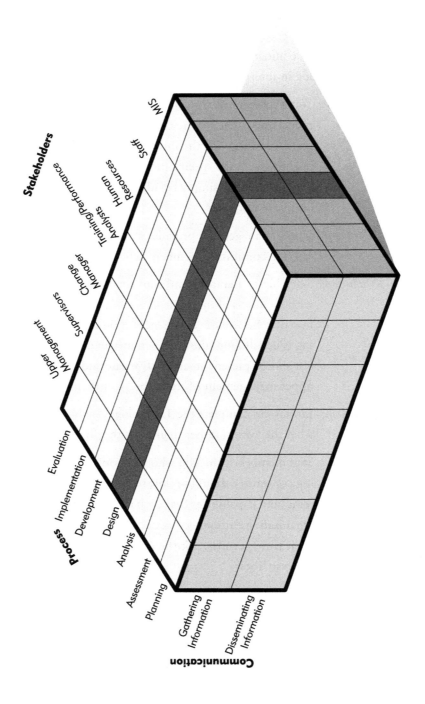

9

Design

THE DESIGN OF A CHANGE INITIATIVE provides the structure by which you can proceed in a systematic manner. In this phase, you expand the critical issues, put them into training and non-training components, and define the results of the change.

Inputs

The input of this phase is a report explaining how to bridge the existing gap.

Outputs

The output is a completed initiative design with clearly defined objectives that will be used to measure the effectiveness of the change.

Responsibilities/Activities

Table 9.1 describes the responsibilities for each of the stakeholders during the Design phase.

Table 9.1. Responsibilities During Design.

Design

Upper Management
- Validate link between global mission and vision
- Approve the Design Report

Change Manager
- Coordinate Design phase activities
- Coordinate completing the Project Management Tool
- Complete Project Assessment Tool
- Monitor schedule and budget
- Complete Evaluation Plan
- Complete final Initiative Design Report

Human Resources
- Coordinate interdepartmental exchange of impacted groups
- Assist in realignment of employees

Management Information Services
- Design any required systems

Supervisors
- Provide inputs to the design of the system with logistics requirements
- Support interdepartmental exchanges

Training/Performance Analysts
- Teach design activities needed for initiative
- Coordinate Evaluation Plan
- Write performance objectives for the initiative
- Complete an Instructional Analysis
- Search for outside sources of expertise for company meetings

Staff
- Provide inputs on design of the initiative from users' viewpoint

Shared Responsibilities
- Complete Project Management Tool
- Provide input into performance objectives
- Participate in Instructional Analysis
- Participate in completing Initiative Design
- Participate in completing the Project Assessment Tool
- Participate in completing the Evaluation Plan
- Support and participate in interdepartmental exchanges.

Upper Management

The change manager should present the completed Design plan to upper management in the form of a Design Report. Once upper management is satisfied that the change initiative objectives adequately link to the company's mission and vision statements, they must approve the report so the initiative can move forward.

Supervisors

Supervisors on the steering committee should give input on the components of the design of the initiative. Supervisors must look at the overall interaction with all affected departments within the supplier-customer framework. This is true on an internal basis as much as it is on an external one. The plan must provide the products and services to customers so that each department can perform its function and receive products and services in a form and within a time frame that meets their needs.

Change Manager

The change manager must lead the change steering committee in completing the Project Assessment Tool and Evaluation Plan to determine how to measure the effect of the change. He or she must coordinate the elements and activities that occur during the Design phase. He or she should review and revise the Project Management Tool for this phase with input from all steering committee members. The change manager must monitor the schedule and budget to be certain that each piece of the design falls in place at the proper time. He or she submits the Design Report to upper management.

Training/Performance Analysts

Training/performance analysts must provide instruction on how to complete a Design plan. They are responsible for writing the objectives for the change initiative (with input from the steering committee) to be certain that they are measurable and that they match the information obtained from Analysis.

Training/performance analysts must search for outside sources of expertise identified during Analysis to fill gaps in the skill sets of current employees if it is not feasible for the organization to develop these skills among existing employees due to complexity, time constraints, or both. These new skills will be needed to implement the change initiative.

Human Resources

The change initiative can impact the way the organization conducts its work, as well as who performs each of the necessary tasks and activities. The change initiative might necessitate a fundamental shakeup in departmental and division alignments, as well as affect supervisory scope. Human Resources professionals use the Analysis Report to redirect employees.

Moving to new groups or interfacing with new work groups can cause apprehension among employees. The best way to eliminate or reduce this apprehension is for HR to provide opportunities for exchanges between the departments that will be impacted. These exchanges should primarily be social, but should be structured in such a way that employees can easily interact rather than cluster into their own familiar groups. These exchanges may be in the form of an orientation to the change initiative that requires individuals from the various groups to work together on an issue, such as imagining how the organization will look after the change.

Why start these exchanges during the Design phase? The sooner that potentially merging groups interact and get to know each other informally, or at least semiformally, the sooner they will become comfortable with the fact that the people in these groups share common interests, just as peers in their original groups did. Therefore, these exchanges facilitate establishing relationships in the new group.

Staff

The staff members on the committee provide inputs to the design from the end-user's point of view. Their input includes whether the solution will meet the objectives of the initiative, making the workforce more efficient, reducing cycle time, and reducing complaints, among others.

Management Information Services

The technical professionals begin to design any required systems that the organization cannot purchase. Those systems that will be purchased must eventually be installed, and these technologists have the responsibility to oversee how that will be done effectively and efficiently.

Shared Responsibilities

Everyone must participate in providing inputs to the Design phase in order to produce the complete outline of the initiative. This participation includes input to the Instructional Analysis of all aspects of the proposed solution and input to the objectives for the initiative. Staff members on the committee should advertise and encourage others in their departments to attend the interdepartmental exchanges. They must also take the lead in introducing members of their group to the committee members of the other groups who, in turn, will introduce them to the members of their own staff groups.

All committee members must also update the Project Management Tool and complete the Project Assessment Tool. This is also the phase where the committee determines how they are going to quantifiably measure the level of effectiveness of the change during evaluation, which is laid out in the Evaluation Plan.

Procedure for Conducting an Instructional Analysis

An Instructional Analysis identifies the specific skills that the organization requires in order to complete and support the change initiative and how these skills will be taught to employees. A well-structured Instructional Analysis should examine the results of all your other analyses and all relevant issues that may involve acquiring new skills. For each issue you analyze, you should identify the required specific knowledge and skills and how employees will acquire them. Examples of how skills will be developed may include training, coaching, or providing online help systems, among others.

Use the Instructional Analysis Tool in Exhibit 9.1 to record your analysis data.

Procedure for Completing a Project Assessment

It is extremely important that you segment the issues in the change initiative that you have identified from the Analysis phase into training elements and

Exhibit 9.1. Instructional Analysis Tool.

Issue:	
Skills Required	How Skill Will Be Provided
1.	
2.	
3.	
4.	
5.	
6.	
7.	
8.	
9.	
10.	
11.	
12.	
13.	
14.	

non-training elements. Exhibit 9.2, the Project Assessment Tool (adapted from Lee & Owens, 2000) provides you a means to structure the information for the initiative. The tool allows you to segment information into three basic levels: systemic, performance, and training.

- *Systemic* issues are those that are basically controlled by upper management and are overarching issues that touch all aspects of the change initiative.

- *Performance* issues are those that will allow stakeholders to do their jobs better once the change occurs.

Exhibit 9.2. Project Assessment Tool.

Level	Category	Definition	Findings
Systemic	Corporate Culture	Will the corporate culture support the solution you propose? • Respect for the individual • Leadership style of management • Acceptance and use of employee ideas	
	Retention	Is keeping valuable and experienced employees a high priority?	
	Incentives	Are users motivated by the organization to use the solution you propose? • Pay structure • Bonuses • Recognition • Performance reviews	
	Organizational Structure	Is structure horizontal or vertical? • Hierarchical structure of the organization • Decision-making authority • Empowered employees • Levels of approval authority	
	Communication	Are people informed of what, how, and why decisions are made? Do people receive feedback?	
Performance	Tools	Do employees have the required equipment to complete their jobs? • Computers • Software • Forms	
	Work Environment	Does the environment where work is done permit people to do their jobs? • On-the-job training after or in place of formal training • Removal of old systems • Coaching • Management support for solution • Temperature • Ventilation	

(*Continued*)

Exhibit 9.2. Project Assessment Tool. (*Continued*)

Level	Category	Definition	Findings
	Processes and Procedures	Do employees understand ways to get their jobs done? • Are there processes and procedures in place for employees to follow? Do employees know whom internal/external customers and partners are? • What are the interdependencies between people/groups to complete work? Are ways of getting work done effective? • Are there too many steps? • Are there unnecessary steps? • Are there unnecessary delays?	
	Expectations	Do employees know what constitutes a job well-done? • Emphasis is on quality • Emphasis is on quantity	
Training	Knowledge	Do employees have the information they need to get the job done?	
	Skills	Do employees have the ability to do their jobs?	
	Attitudes	Do employees know the importance of doing their jobs?	

Adapted from W. Lee & D. Owens, *Multimedia-Based Instructional Design: Computer-Based Training, Web-Based Training, Distance Broadcast Training* (San Francisco: Jossey-Bass/Pfeiffer, 2000).

- *Training* issues are the knowledge, skills, and attitudes that will be required to support the change.

At the systemic level, the tool considers the following elements:

- *Corporate Culture*—The value an organization places on its people, partners, and customers;

- *Retention*—Employee turnover in an organization;

- *Incentives*—The organization's reward system;

- *Organizational Structure*—Whether the hierarchy is vertical with many levels and many decision-making levels or whether people are empowered to make decisions about their own jobs; and

- *Communication*—The way that information flows up and down in the organization, determining the method and the quantity of information shared.

Examining performance issues requires the discovery of the following elements:

- *Tools*—The equipment available to accomplish work;

- *Work Environment*—The physical conditions under which people do their work;

- *Processes and Procedures*—The systematic methodologies in place that inform employees how to accomplish their work; and

- *Expectations*—Criteria that constitute the perceived standards for a task or job.

Training is the transfer of:

- *Knowledge*—The information inherent in the change;

- *Skills*—The physical capabilities required to change; and

- *Attitudes*—The belief that the change is beneficial to the employees and to the organization.

Addressing each element discovered during the organizational assessment begins in one of the following places: At the *highest level* (systemic) working downward to specific training issues that might be required and, at *each level,* simultaneously addressing common elements at each level.

Procedure for Writing Objectives

After completing the Project Assessment Tool, your next step is to write objectives for each issue identified (Lee & Owens, 2000). Exhibit 9.3 is a form you can use for this purpose.

Exhibit 9.3. Objectives Worksheet.

Level	Category	Objective
Systemic	Corporate Culture	
	Retention	
	Incentives	
	Organizational Structure	
	Communication	
Performance	Tools	
	Work Environment	
	Processes and Procedures	
	Expectations	
Training	Knowledge	
	Skills	
	Attitudes	

Objectives should be:

Outcome based, not behaviorally based	Initiative objectives should state what the initiative's end accomplishments should achieve, not the activities required in order to get there (individual work committees should write these activity objectives).
Specific	All objectives should state specific outcomes.
Measurable	All objectives should include components that allow you to tell when they are accomplished because you can measure an impact.

Agreed on by everyone	Not only should the change steering committee agree to the objectives, but upper management must also agree on them. Ideally, the committee and upper management should write these jointly. However, if upper management delegates the task to the change steering committee, management should at least "sign off" on them. We believe that objectives should never be written by either group separately and handed to the other. Nor should only one or two members of the change steering committee write the objectives. By having everyone agree to the objectives, there is ownership by everyone.
Realistic	The accomplishments must be realistic. This means that affected employees should be able to complete them in a reasonable period of time. They should reflect a challenge, but neither be too easy nor too difficult to achieve.
Timed	You should set deadlines by which each objective will be accomplished.

Here is an example of a mission statement and properly written objectives:

Company X will install a new telecommunications system.
The objectives are as follows:

1. **The initiative committee will have chosen a new telecommunications system for Company X by January 1, 2004.**

2. **All departments within the company transitioned to accept and use the new telecommunications system by May 1, 2005.**

3. **The company will implement the use of the new telecommunications system by May 15, 2005.**

4. **The MIS department will monitor the implementation of the new telecommunications system until May 30, 2005, to ensure successful integration.**

5. **The company will establish financial criteria for suitability of a telecommunication system for Company X by March 1, 2004.**

6. **The MIS department will locate at least five sources of telecommunication systems vendors and evaluate them by April 1, 2004.**

7. **The committee will make its recommendation for the selected system by October 2004.**

Evaluation Plan

Measurable objectives are the basis of the Evaluation Plan. You can now map the objectives to the Skill Gap Analysis Tool (Exhibit 8.1). At this point you need to develop an Evaluation Plan to outline how you will determine the return on investment (ROI) for the change. The tools for completing the Evaluation Plan and Evaluation Report are in Chapter 12 (see Exhibit 12.2). During this phase, you will complete Section II; the remaining sections will be completed during the Evaluation phase.

The Design Report

All of the completed tools during the Design phase comprise the Design Report. The change manager must combine the tools into one structured format and present the report to upper management.

CASE STUDY 1
DESIGN

Armed with the information from the Analysis phase, the change steering committee went to work on the exact design of the initiative. At the end of this phase they would need a completely outlined plan for implementing the system, with content specified for each aspect of the initiative. As usual, Jess began the phase by updating the Project Management Tool with the change steering committee and asked Joy to share budget information with everyone.

The change to an SAP system represented more than just activities in checking, purchasing, and installing equipment and computer programs. Indeed, the fundamental nature of how and which employees did what type of work was subject to change. Remember that one of the benefits of using an SAP system is to eliminate redundancies and increase efficiencies as well as effectiveness. Marcia Morgan, the HR director, began an intensive investigation as to how these changes impacted the structure of the organization and the reporting relationships among key players. At first, the change put some entire jobs in jeopardy. For example, because sales volume data under SAP would not be guarded by one department that allowed employees to obtain figures only on request, the organization did not need fully half of the employees in Marketing Services. Many employees could simply access the figures whenever they wished. Further, since the SAP system allowed much freer access to documents, messages, reports, and archived documents, the physical activity that previously required several employees to access, authorize, and distribute information could now be accomplished by just one person who served in a "gate-keeping" function.

Perhaps the most revealing data available to the change steering committee were the apprehensions and fears expressed by the users themselves. Some of these became apparent through formal memos or conversations in departmental meetings; others were simply rumors shared between two employees on an informal basis. The list ran the gamut. For example, "Why does the purchasing department get new computers when ours are three years older than theirs?" "I don't want to learn another system." "It took me two years to figure out what I'm doing right now. I don't have time nor the desire to figure out something new."

The change steering committee examined the positive and negative consequences of implementing the plan as it designed the initiative. They determined that overall positive effects would accrue by a more integrated approach to communicating with other departments, as well as by an increase in the level and speed of communication, and just by doing business. The negative aspects of the plan were that some people, those who could not adapt to the technology, might become lost and disenfranchised. However, HR's plan provided liberal severance packages, including training and job avenues for these people to move to other departments in the company that were not affected by the change.

Because SAP would eventually find its way throughout the entire corporation, including field employees and company-owned stores, the committee decided that, because of the complexity, those members who designed and developed the plan would have to continue working with the initiative until it was fully implemented. They then added the requirement that they work for a period of at least a year thereafter to monitor SAP usage to be certain that departments did not slip in their efficiency.

Capital expenditure budgets of $3.2 million were allocated for the conversion. The change steering committee was charged with the responsibility of determining the order in which each department would submit maps of its various processes, receive new or upgraded equipment, and then "go live" on SAP. Training/performance analysis professionals arranged for users to learn the new software and computer methods on a priority basis.

One important contribution in this phase was that each change steering committee member began to carefully develop written objectives that applied to his or her department or division's aspect of the change. They did this with inputs from selected members from their department or division. Each department was asked to construct revised objectives for their work divisions that were consistent with those of the organization. Training/performance analysts were enlisted to assist any managers who had difficulty writing their objectives or linking them to those of the larger organization.

One manager, Bill Jackson, who had been a supervisor in the company's order entry department for five years, experienced particular difficulty in writing objectives that were truly "ends" or "products," as opposed to activities. For example, one of his objectives was for all of his employees to "understand the process to retrieve customer sales data slices." After some coaching by training/performance analysts, this objective was altered to read "produce weekly year-to-date (YTD) budget spreadsheets for each customer in Excel spreadsheets from customer sales data slices." This objective specified the exact measurable standards to judge whether or not the objective was achieved.

This was a busy phase for Jess Albertson. While it took approximately six weeks for Blumroth to pass through this phase, Jess was so busy he felt at though a year had gone by. He attended countless meetings, repeated the same answer to the same question hundreds of times, and maintained an optimistic demeanor through-out. He managed to coordinate all of his activities with the help of the rest of the committee.

Upper management examined the objectives from each of the divisions to be certain that they were all linked to the organizational goals, and the committee examined them to be sure that they matched the initiative mission statement. In some cases, training/performance analysts provided some help in refining objectives.

Human Resources began to search for external sources for training required for the mapping sessions, as well as skills to use SAP correctly. In their conversations with training/performance analysts, the two departments agreed that screen prints from some of the process mapping used for input into SAP would also become excellent job aids and materials for training new users. MIS began the process for pricing and purchasing the required hardware and software. They determined the exact specifications that were needed to upgrade each computer station. Users who would need networks to share information were scheduled for hookups. MIS was also very careful about scheduling the installation of SAP in ways that were consistent with the workflow of a department and, specifically, how it was connected to the work of other departments, either as an input or output in a process.

Supervisors provided a great deal of input to the technical professionals concerning specifications about job requirements and functions that employees would have to perform, whether continued or modified, once the company implemented SAP. In some cases, these conversations provided the greatest and most comical communication challenges, as the users spoke technical language about their own job specifications while the technical professionals used specific jargon that was not understood by the users. Therefore, the two groups had to get together and develop some common terminology. Finally, all processes, procedures, and work instructions were documented. The supervisors also began initiating some of the sessions with employees to capture the current processes in mapping sessions. At first, most supervisors attempted to complete one process per day. Once the employees began to increase their comfort level with mapping procedures, the pace and frequency for these sessions improved.

Each committee member had to keep the mission and objectives paramount. The most critical factor was not which department received what equipment or who trained which users on which skills, but, rather, whether the work objectives and company vision and mission were being fulfilled by the activities undertaken. In several cases, MIS employees appealed to the change steering committee to decide whether a request was truly a "need" or just a "want."

After six weeks Jess and his committee had a good handle on the objectives and the activities that would be needed to implement the plan. Now they were ready to develop the plan into a full-blown implementation strategy in order that Blumroth could proceed with the pilot.

CASE STUDY 2
DESIGN

From the information gathered during the Analysis phase, the change steering committee could proceed with designing the restructuring of the organization. The key feature of the output of the Design phase is a completely outlined plan, with objectives to measure the effectiveness of the change. The first step that Cherie took in this phase with the change steering committee was to revise and update the Project Management Tool.

In order to get a good feel for the process, Cherie asked the committee members to write objectives based on the outcomes of the Analysis phase. She also reminded everyone of the vision and mission statements from the Assessment phase. Specifically, the committee wrote training, performance, and systemic objectives that the organization had to achieve in order to bridge the gap, in accordance with the Project Assessment Tool. (You can read samples of these objectives at the end of this section.) Cherie asked them to be sure that the objectives were specific performance outcomes based on analysis data and that they took into account possible impact from the restructuring in the organization. She reminded everyone that she would submit the completed design plan to upper management, whose major concern would be how tightly aligned the objectives were with the findings from Analysis.

In the change steering committee meetings, Lynn Davis continued to provide some techniques to improve the way the group worked together. She occasionally completed the Group Interaction Analysis during a meeting and reported findings to help the committee work in an effective manner. Some of the committee members remarked that they had been using a few of Lynn's tips and techniques to improve their own meetings with their staff and peers.

In order to ensure continuity throughout the organization, the change steering committee then asked each department to consider writing objectives as well. Members of the change steering committee offered assistance to any departments that had difficulty completing the task and, in most cases, the assistance provided was not based on lack of understanding of the process, but rather on a lack of agreement among employees as to what the objectives should cover.

This was an important phase for Marv and the training/performance analysts. The objectives that come out of this phase served as the anchors for the training that resulted from the Instructional Analysis. Not only would these objectives allow for gaps and strengths in skills to be identified, but also the department would need to identify in which areas it was not capable of providing services and, therefore, would need to locate external resources. Cherie asked Marv to serve as the unofficial "clearing" person to screen, review, and clarify objectives as department managers finished them.

The magnitude of the change initiative became clearer after the change steering committee reviewed the results from the Instructional Analysis. The most significant finding from this phase was the awesome amount of knowledge that the organization would need to help the employees become competent in the way that they would perform their jobs. Whether the subject was a salesperson (who needed to learn about products new to him or her in order to be successful in selling) or an accountant (who needed to learn about new processes specific to types of customers) or an HR professional (who needed to learn the component activities of jobs he or she had never dealt with), the knowledge and skill gaps were enormous. In some cases, employees were proficient in "transferable" skills and simply needed to learn how to apply these in new contexts. In other cases, employees had never acquired, nor had they practiced, the skills that they would be using as their jobs changed.

Instructional Analysis revealed that external, "off-the-shelf" training programs, whether face-to-face or online, would be woefully inadequate to produce the level of skills necessary for Northcutt to obtain the outcomes that it required. This analysis gave Marv "fuel for the fire" for his argument to allow existing managers and employees to train others on a cross-functional basis in the knowledge and skills required to perform their jobs.

Marv was convinced that if the corporation undertook the task of filling this gap in a cross-functional way, the company would save a considerable amount of money from hiring external sources, and also the employees who trained others would be far more involved and committed to the change. He presented these ideas to the change steering committee and, after listening to some reservations, overcame the objections by suggesting that many employees actually enjoy teaching and coaching others and would do well at it. His responses moved the idea forward. The challenge was then to identify who needed training, who could provide the training, and the best method for doing it.

Bruce was particularly interested in the role that human resources played during this phase. Since the proposed reorganization required employees to work with new people and coordinate new activities, Bruce believed that the change steering committee should endorse initial exchanges between employees in groups that would later interact regularly, if not actually work together. In response, Cherie asked the change steering committee members to consider topics that would be important for the reorganized company to consider that these people could meet about and discuss. Many of the committee members believed that these employees should not meet just to get to know one another, but rather, to actually talk about and work on important issues that could impact the organization in the near future.

After Marv, Cherie, and, ultimately, the entire change steering committee reviewed the objectives that the different divisions and departments offered, she submitted the Design Report to upper management to obtain their endorsement as well as their views about how well the objectives linked to the organizational goals, mission, and vision statement. After making some modifications, she prepared a draft of the Evaluation Plan for the change steering committee to review.

As part of the Design phase report, Bruce decided that the pilot test of the change would be held with the western zone. Each salesperson would be asked to implement the plan by meeting new customers, reviewing existing business, and selling all of the products. This zone would only have a four-week lead on the rest of the company, but the feedback that they provided would be useful to the other zones prior to their implementation of the reorganization.

The western zone salespeople would be asked to deliver voice-mail summaries twice per day during the pilot for feedback concerning customer receptivity. The company would hire contractors to transcribe this feedback and provide it to the training/ performance analysts, who would then do a formative evaluation with the data. The outcome was to determine the kinds of customer reactions, unanticipated issues, and problems that the salespeople encountered working in this new way. The plan was for Marv and his team to transfer any feedback to the vice presidents of the other three zones daily so that they could make appropriate adjustments for their own launches.

The committee paid the greatest amount of attention in this phase to the Instructional Analysis and the Project Assessment tools. Due to his expertise in this area, Marv led the committee through the Instructional Analysis. For every objective submitted by a departmental or divisional manager, the committee gathered a list of the skills required by an employee to achieve the objective and then a corresponding note of how the organization would provide the skill. Everyone on the committee recognized the importance of completing the Instructional Analysis correctly. Since the change initiative for Northcutt involved an extensive shuffling of employees performing new skills and working with new responsibilities, it was imperative for the committee to accurately identify the skills that these employees would need to perform in order to achieve the objectives. The committee was already well aware that many employees would not already be proficient in these skills; therefore, the organization needed to ensure the availability of methods to provide the training.

The Project Assessment Tool identified all of the facets that the organization had to adjust or accommodate in order to make the objectives work. In most cases for Northcutt, completing the tool identified not so much items that the company needed to acquire or change, but rather things that employees would have to become accustomed to in their new roles and responsibilities. For example, a performance issue identified was that all of the departments that belonged to one silo would undergo significant cultural and work environment changes when collapsed into single entities at the Kansas City headquarters. Many employees would need to abandon long-performed tasks and learn new ones. Before signing off on the tool, the committee reviewed the contents with the specific department managers in order to ensure accuracy. A training issue involved how employees would acquire the skills. A systemic issue was the realignment along customer lines rather than product lines.

Translated into sample objectives published in the Design Report, these three issues read as follows:

- *Systemic*—**Northcutt will obtain the same level of customer satisfaction after the reorganization that it achieved prior to the reorganization.**

- *Training*—**Northcutt salespeople will deliver thirty-second presentations focused on all four products.**

- *Performance*—**Northcutt will make online assistance available for employees to access to execute company software programs.**

Other results published in the Design Report were that training was to be delivered online by providing new product information to sales and marketing and that processes and procedures would be put into online performance support systems. As needed, various managers and others would post updated bulletins on the corporate intranet. The design called for all sales and marketing personnel to be brought in for a two-day meeting to share customer information. Customer product information would be placed online so that salespeople could hook into customers' computer systems to provide the most updated information on products and services—and even go online at a customer site to provide information.

On a Wednesday, Bruce and Cherie met with various executives in small groups to draft a clear presentation containing the rationale for making the change, along with a clear delineation of the potential positive outcomes and risks. Once they had gathered and organized all of the information, they asked Marie Bulton, an internal graphics designer, to produce PowerPoint slides that they could use on Friday for the presentation.

As a result of the committee's hard work, Cherie and the change steering committee had a plan and believed that they were ready with the components required for the change.

What Could Go Wrong

In this phase, you need to be prepared for unanticipated problems, such as:

Problem: The change initiative appears to require more time to prepare for implementation than upper management desires.

Solution: You may consider adding more people to the change steering committee, establishing additional subcommittees or task forces, or even hiring additional employees or contractors. These options will likely impact the change initiative budget. You may also wish to consider eliminating certain steps in a phase, although we do not advocate doing so due to the risk of not implementing the initiative correctly.

Problem: In spite of training, some people do not write objectives correctly.

Solution: This is a skill that some people find more difficult to do correctly than others. If, after training, the skill level for some people who are required to write objectives does not improve, one option is to delegate the task to another person.

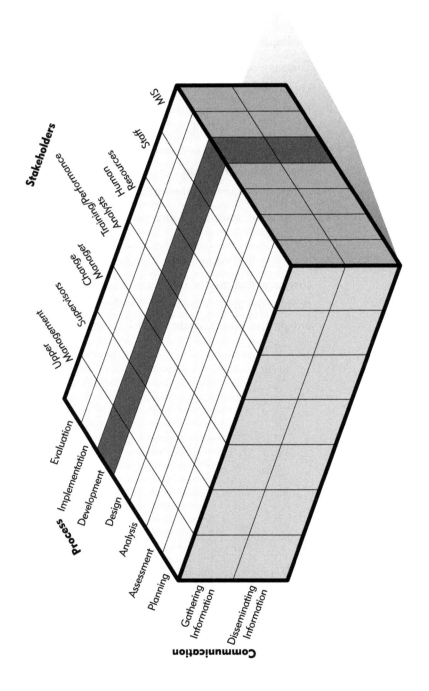

10

Development

IN THIS PHASE, the Design Report becomes a fully conceived initiative-ready for implementation.

Inputs

The input is a completed initiative design with clearly defined objectives that will be used to measure the effectiveness of the change.

Outputs

The output of this phase is a fully developed initiative containing all of the logistical and material components that must be put into effect.

Responsibilities/Activities

Table 10.1 includes a listing of the responsibilities of each stakeholder group during the Development phase.

Upper Management

Upper management is always busy with important corporate responsibilities throughout the process of the change initiative. Upper management has no direct responsibilities during this phase, but they do have shared responsibilities with the other stakeholder groups. Their "non-involvement" at this point in the process is very positive. It actually shows support and trust in the change steering committee.

Table 10.1. Responsibilities During Development.

Development	
Upper Management • No direct responsibilities (all covered under Shared Responsibilities)	**Supervisors** • Begin examining operational schedules to provide release time for training and the pilot study • Provide inputs to the development of the system with logistics requirements
Change Manager • Coordinate Development phase • Coordinate completing the Project Management Tool • Complete the Project Plan • Coordinate company meetings • Monitor schedule and budget	**Training/Performance Analysts** • Teach Development phase activities • Develop learning strategies for acquiring skills required for the implementation of the change • Schedule training
Human Resources • Develop career ladders and attrition plans • Schedule external resources to speak at company and interdepartmental meetings	**Staff** • Keep peers informed of initiative progress and implications • Write releases and memos
Management Information Services • Test and debug selected systems and/or develop new systems	**Shared Responsibilities** • Complete Project Management Tool for this phase • Support company meetings • Carry out assigned objectives • Review initiative progress

Supervisors

Supervisors must keep their peers informed of the progress of the initiative with respect to the way that the daily operations of their direct reports will be affected. They must also examine operational schedules to provide release time for training/performance analysts to train their employees on new skills required. They should also work with MIS on the match between the components of systems and the logistical requirements that the change will affect.

Change Manager

The change manager is responsible for coordinating all of the activities in this phase and completing the Project Management Tool. He or she must put the Project Plan in place (see Exhibit 10.1), coordinate any company meetings, and monitor the schedule to ensure that all activities proceed in a timely manner and adhere to the budget.

Exhibit 10.1. Project Plan.

Initiative Title:
Initiative Team Members [names of all committee members and their roles]:
Initiative Goal [statement of the overall purpose of the initiative]:
Commissioned by [group sponsoring the initiative]:
Executive Summary [a one-page statement of what is going to happen to complete the initiative]
Note that each objective should be on a separate page so it can be distributed to the person responsible for completing it.
Initiative Objective: Issue Addressed: Tasks Required: Consulted: Informed: Date to Be Completed: Date of Completion:

(Continued)

Exhibit 10.1. Project Plan. (*Continued*)

Initiative Objective:
Issue Addressed:
Tasks Required:
Responsible:
Consulted:
Informed:
Date to Be Completed:
Date of Completion:
Initiative Objective:
Issue Addressed:
Tasks Required:
Responsible:
Consulted:
Informed:
Date to Be Completed:
Date of Completion:
Initiative Objective:
Issue Addressed:
Tasks Required:
Responsible:
Consulted:
Informed:
Date to Be Completed:
Date of Completion:
Initiative Objective:
Issue Addressed:
Tasks Required:
Responsible:
Consulted:
Informed:
Date to Be Completed:
Date of Completion:

The Project Management Tool assigns the roles and responsibilities for each phase. The Project Plan is task-specific and links to objectives, issues, and expected results developed during the Analysis phase.

Training/Performance Analysts

Training professionals develop and schedule the training and other forms of skill acquisition that are required for the new competencies. This involves prioritizing who learns which skills and when they are trained. They also identify what is required, along with the exact content of each intervention.

Human Resources

Since any change in the organization likely produces changes in the basic work of the company as well, HR professionals must consider the impact of the change on the work that is performed as well as on the people who perform it. For instance, many changes that involve technological advances have a profound effect on manpower in an organization. As a result of these changes, HR must develop career ladders and attrition plans for the employees who are affected by the change initiative. For those who are leaving the company, this means severance packages that will allow them to retrain for a new career in the workforce. For those who remain with the company, HR must write and prepare transfer papers, promotion papers, and new job descriptions and put these into place upon implementation of the change initiative.

There is a hierarchy of options that should be considered when downsizing is necessary. The first should be voluntary options such as early retirement. Next should be voluntary resignations with a severance package. Use involuntary reductions only as a last resort when job skills are no longer required and employees cannot fill jobs with new skill requirements. Remember the research we cited in the Introduction that only 25 percent of all companies that downsized in order to achieve productivity gains ever achieved them. Involuntarily released employees should also receive a severance package.

It is also HR's job to schedule speakers from outside the company who have experience with change initiatives to speak at company and initiative meetings and interdepartmental exchanges.

Staff

Staff representatives on the change steering committee must keep their peers informed of what changes are evolving so they can be prepared for the training and the changes that will occur. The staff communications specialist writes memos and other releases about the initiative.

Management Information Services

Technical professionals must not only test existing systems with employees but develop new ones as well. If the change effort can be placed in a test mode before the pilot test in order to determine what "bugs" exist, the transition into the change effort will be much smoother.

Shared Responsibilities

All change steering committee members must participate in reviews of the components of the initiative as they are developed. This allows them to be certain that each component aligns with the objectives for the change initiative. They also need to ensure that the components being developed align as designed, all of which must fit into the change initiative mission statement as well as the company's mission and vision statements. All committee members also have the responsibility to complete the Project Management Tool for this phase.

CASE STUDY 1
DEVELOPMENT

As the company entered the Development phase, it had a completely outlined plan with the exact activities and functions noted for each aspect of the change. Now the committee completed the Project Plan, adding each duty, activity, and step that had to be taken—and in the correct order.

After updating the Project Management Tool, the change steering committee decided that three departments would pilot SAP. The departments chosen all accessed the same type of data, and inputs from one group frequently served as outputs for another group. The three selected departments were Accounting, Order Entry, and Inventory Control. Managers from New Product Development and Corporate Communications voiced the loudest objections to not being selected for the pilot, but the change steering committee held with its original selection.

Jess continued to coordinate the activities of the change steering committee along with the activities of teams throughout the organization as they prepared to make the conversion.

The MIS team began to purchase and install the new hardware and software according to the schedule and began to develop the systems that the company would need to put it all together. Users who had to share documents and spreadsheets with each other through SAP needed to have the same available features and be on the same network.

The change steering committee established a deadline for all mapped processes to be submitted, and the response rate was better than 90 percent. Some change steering committee members had to "prod" some departments to finish, and the training/performance analysts had to supply facilitators to some sessions in order that a department could work through conflicts or problems regarding a process.

While everyone was busy, training/performance analysts worked with the external SAP consulting specialists the company hired to bring them up-to-speed on the requirements and ensure the quality of the training. Steve, the training/performance analysis steering committee member, sat through dry runs of some of the training sessions in order to evaluate the quality and applicability of the instruction. Some sessions were basic, such as accessing the system and maneuvering through various screens. Other sessions were more advanced, including modifying profiles, preparing a multivariate search, and establishing schedules for automatic report generation. Some of the training was also developed internally, especially for modifying company-specific templates and applications to fit SAP. Blumroth purchased some training in the form of self-study; some was computer-based training.

MIS worked to determine how the documented procedures and work instructions would work in the new SAP environment. They had to account for the numerous differences in the processes, along with the way they were executed. They made all of the necessary modifications to the SAP-supplied documentation and distributed information to various departments in printed form, in downloadable .pdf files, and in read-only .txt files. The members of the affected departments were trained on the new systems using the documented procedures.

Human Resources brought in people from other companies that had made the same change and had them speak at company meetings. They used these testimonials to defuse those few employees who still said: "It won't work here." One testimonial came from Howard Stein, CEO of Monroe Davis Tax Systems, while another came from Hal Kuehn, a sales manager from Caterpillar, USA. These two people were so sold on SAP and so happy with the efficiencies that the initiative had brought to their companies that many at Blumroth began to talk positively about the change.

With the implementation plan fully developed, the company was ready to initiate the pilot for the three selected departments.

CASE STUDY 2
DEVELOPMENT

The committee's attention now focused on the material and logistical components necessary for the change initiative to be successful. This required the committee to consider the specific changes in the proper sequence in order to launch the change initiative.

As with other phases, Cherie's initial meeting with the change steering committee was to review and update the Project Management Tool in order to confirm responsibilities for this phase. The committee also reviewed and discussed the Project Plan. Cherie also discussed the status of the budget for the initiative with the committee members. MIS was particularly antsy about having enough money to test and debug all of the modifications to the technology systems that the change initiative required due to consolidation.

Human Resources professionals had already started talking with vice presidents, directors, and managers in the various departments affected by the organization in order to identify, on a preliminary basis, which employees would be best suited to take which positions and perform what work under the reorganization. Although HR did not hold any conversations with employees during this phase, they did begin to pull together potential numbers of employees who would be needed in the various jobs, along with the number who would need transfers, as well as those who would likely lose their jobs. The only task that would remain after this phase would be to talk with the specific employees the company wanted to "stay on board," but who would be affected by the reorganization, to see whether they wanted to continue to work for Northcutt under the new arrangements. Some of the finance managers provided input on relocation costs while HR was deciding on a firm that specialized in these services in order to outsource those functions to them. Human Resources also began to hold preliminary conversations with executives from local outplacement firms, in preparation for employees who chose to separate from the company using their services.

The technology professionals in management information services were very busy during this phase in identifying the modifications that had to be made to various programs in order to accomplish the centralization of work for numerous departments in the corporate headquarters. While they certainly did not need to start over with anything, they realized that there was a considerable amount of work to do to reroute files and to change which employee groups and individuals would have access to systems on the server. The change steering committee received some fearful input about companies that did not block out access to systems early enough prior to layoffs and had found that some angry employees attempted to sabotage the system. Since the company had extensive backup for all of its servers, this was not a major concern, although it could have been a nuisance if it happened at Northcutt. In some cases, MIS professionals had to requisition the purchase of some new hardware and software in order that they could test it prior to the implementation of the pilot portion of the change initiative. Staff committee members continued to coordinate the activities of the change steering committee and also the activities of teams throughout the organization as they prepared to make the conversion.

In this phase, Marv identified a number of external training firms that could provide reassigned workers the skills identified through the Project Assessment Tool as being needed to perform their jobs well. While the majority of the training would be delivered online, there were certain skills that required a traditional classroom setting. Without naming anyone specifically who would remain with the company, be transferred, or laid off, the company began to prepare to schedule employees who needed to complete skill training. Marv and a few other trainers agreed to personally participate in some of the online and classroom sessions in order to get a feel for how well the external firms were delivering their product. In some cases, Marv already had lined up Northcutt's own internal trainers to provide the training. In other cases, the change steering committee had already authorized the purchase of online and CD-ROM programs to allow employees to become proficient in skills they would need.

Human Resources' plan was structured in three phases. First, the company offered voluntary early retirement at age fifty to those with twenty years' experience. Second, Northcutt asked for voluntary separations with a package based on years of experience (one month's pay for every year of service, retraining, college tuition payment, and so forth). The third phase called for involuntary separation with the same separation package.

The communication processes continued to be very important for the committee to emphasize to all employees who would remain in their current positions within the organization. Various committee members continued to write updates for the corporate intranet and the company newsletter, highlighting specific actions that Northcutt was taking relative to the change initiative. Over the weeks that preceded this phase, employees posted almost 50 percent fewer questions to the Web site, thus indicating that people were focusing more on their work and less on any unknowns about the change.

Once Cherie and the other change steering committee members were satisfied with the Implementation Plan, especially the determination of which employees would go where, they believed that Northcutt was ready to launch the pilot for the change initiative.

What Could Go Wrong

As always, problems may arise during this phase. In particular, you should be prepared for the following:

Problem: The time it takes to test and debug the systems may take longer than expected, thus potentially delaying the pilot.

Solution: Under these conditions, the change manager and change steering committee must determine whether to abandon plans to run a pilot and move forward to full implementation. We believe that a pilot is an important step to take, because any problems or unexpected issues that arise are contained within the limited boundaries. These problems or issues may become very costly if discovered during a full implementation. The best solution is to extend the timeline for the initiative and make up the extra time and cost by conducting a pilot in two regions, departments, or locations, rather than just one.

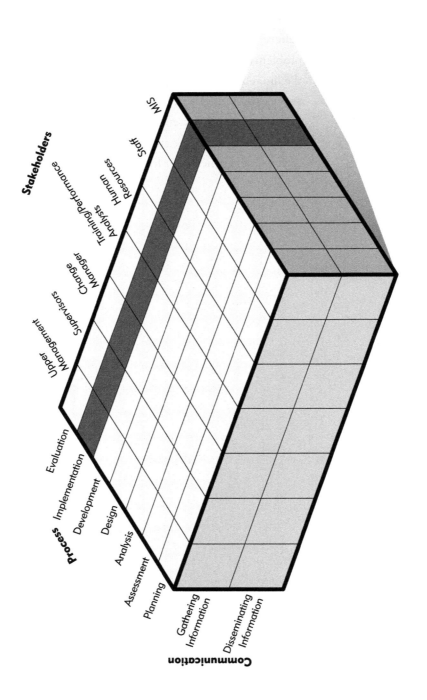

Stakeholders

MIS
Staff
Human Resources
Training/Performance Analysts
Change Manager
Supervisors
Upper Management

Process

Evaluation
Implementation
Development
Design
Analysis
Assessment
Planning

Communication

Gathering Information
Disseminating Information

11

Implementation

IN THIS PHASE, the change steering committee puts the planned change initiative into effect. All required instruction is delivered and all systems are put in place. A small-scale pilot program is completed, followed by full-scale implementation.

Note: We cannot overemphasize the importance of conducting a small pilot. It is unwise to attempt a full-scale implementation without a pilot. The pilot test gives the committee the opportunity to work out any "bugs" and readjust for the full implementation.

Inputs

The input to this phase is a fully developed initiative containing all of the logistical and material components that must be put into effect.

Outputs

The output is an implemented change initiative.

Responsibilities/Activities

The stakeholder responsibilities for the Implementation phase are shown in Table 11.1.

Upper Management

Upper management has no specific responsibilities during this phase. Their responsibilities are covered under Shared Responsibilities below.

Table 11.1. Responsibilities During Implementation.

Implementation

Upper Management • No specific responsibilities (all covered under Shared Responsibilities)	**Supervisors** • Supervise and support those who are participating in the pilot test/full-scale implementation • Report issues about the pilot and implementation to responsible steering committee members for solutions
Change Manager • Coordinate the pilot • Manage full-scale implementation • Coordinate completing the Project Management Tool • Monitor schedule and budget	**Training/Performance Analysts** • Teach Implementation phase activities • Monitor Implementation phase
Human Resources • Implement career ladders and attrition plans	**Staff** • Write releases and memos • Coach and counsel employees to meet individual needs • Become on-the-job trainers • Guide the pilot project
Management Information Services • Monitor and maintain systems during pilot and full-scale implementation	**Shared Responsibilities** • Support pilot and full-scale implementation • Attend meetings • Complete Project Management Tool • Provide feedback to change manager on issues during the pilot and full-scale implementation

Supervisors

Supervisors must be available to employees from their departments who participate in the pilot test. When the change is first implemented, there will be challenges and even frustrations. Supervisors can be of great assistance by listening to staff members—to their problems and difficulties—and providing suggestions for overcoming them. In addition, they must channel the suggestions to the person on the change steering committee who can best resolve them.

Change Manager

The change manager must coordinate all the activities of the pilot test by holding regular meetings with the change steering committee, managing the progress of the pilot and implementation, and working out any problems as they arise. Frequent monitoring will prevent small obstacles from becoming huge problems. The change manager should also inform the entire change steering committee about the progress of the pilot and implementation, complete the Project Management Tool for this phase, and monitor the budget.

Training/Performance Analysts

Training and performance analysts must teach the components of the Implementation phase. These are primarily the logistics of interfacing between groups that the change steering committee decides to coordinate. In addition, however, it involves explaining the processes and procedures involved in conducting the pilot test to the entire change steering committee and those who will participate in the test. These committee members must stay involved during the pilot and the full-scale implementation to provide feedback to participants and to gather, interpret, and report data from the pilot for the purpose of improving the quality of the project.

Human Resources

In this phase, HR must implement the career ladders that they developed for employees to move into and out of the positions. During Implementation, they work with employees to help them schedule and complete the training that will assist them in moving vertically or horizontally through the company.

They must also provide severance packages for those who will leave the company, either through retirement or moving to new jobs with other companies. All of this movement ensures that those who are working with the new program have the necessary skills to do well, along with the attitude required to move the change forward.

Staff

The staff members will work with their departments and train the pilot participants on the procedures and strategies that they must operationalize during the pilot test. Their responsibilities include coaching and counseling pilot participants to meet individual needs and providing feedback on how well they are performing. In this phase, they become the experts on the change initiative and they will be invaluable as on-the-job trainers when the project is fully implemented.

The communications specialist will write memos and releases for the project.

Management Information Services

Technical support needs to monitor and maintain the systems during the pilot test to keep them functioning in order that the implementation of the change initiative stays on schedule. Technologists can determine during the pilot whether the systems are actually robust enough to handle the requirements that a full-scale implementation calls for. If not, the change steering committee may decide to delay full-scale implementation while they examine, test, and install new systems and then conduct another pilot test.

Shared Responsibilities

All committee members must demonstrate verbal and visible support for the pilot and full-scale implementation. They must attend steering committee meetings, complete the Project Management Tool, and provide feedback to the change manager on any issues that arise from their responsibilities during implementation of the change initiative.

CASE STUDY 1
IMPLEMENTATION

The official pilot launch of SAP at Blumroth was filled with excitement, anticipation, and apprehension. After reviewing and updating the Project Management Tool, every change steering committee member was "on pins and needles" waiting to hear about successes. Those individuals who had prepared for the day literally paced the hallways waiting to hear word about how things were going.

Recall that the first departments to go live with SAP were accounting, order entry, and inventory control. Even though the work that they performed was real, a few of the employees actually referred to what they were doing in conversations with others as a small-scale test.

Each department managed to run at least two different types of processes by mid-morning. Various change steering committee members monitored the processes in the various departments. Over the next several days, the committee held regular meetings to discuss problems and make changes to the system, procedures, and work instructions as necessary. The committee also monitored the users' comfort levels and their attitude toward the system. They answered user questions and documented these questions and answers for compilation and distribution before full-scale implementation. The committee also reassured the users that their drop in productivity was only temporary and was to be expected until they really caught on to the new system.

MIS was available to work out bugs as quickly as they were identified. Interestingly, user patience and the ability or inability to simply follow instructions were the biggest obstacles. Other technicians from MIS continued to stay one step ahead of the game. While this pilot was being run in the first three departments, the MIS teams began to install the programs for other users in anticipation of the full-scale implementation within a few weeks.

Training/performance analysts also worked to determine the kinds of issues and questions that frequently recurred from user to user. These were compiled in spreadsheets as an initial reservoir of lessons learned for the purpose of conducting a user-friendly training program on "tips, tricks, and traps." Surprisingly, most of the questions did fall into these categories. There were a few, but not many, questions that made reference to a particular computer or job-specific task, the answers to which were of limited use for preparing others.

The major result from the pilot was the realization that there were a few very complex processes that needed an online job aid to lead users through the procedures. Some issues that users identified were forwarded to the local SAP consultants who had worked with the company from the outset. Since this was not an anticipated need, there was not any money budgeted for constructing customized online help procedures. Jess prepared a proposal, including a rationale for the expenditure, provided it to the change steering committee for reactions, and then forwarded it to the CEO for approval. Because the company had invested so much money in SAP up to this point, this expenditure was minimal, especially considering its usefulness.

The CEO held one company-wide meeting during this phase. At this time, he not only covered third-quarter profits and new policies, but also encouraged employees to become mentors to coach and counsel other users as they became accustomed to the new system. This was particularly important as positions and personnel changed. Such words were music to the ears of Jess and his change steering committee, for they truly underscored the team approach to managing this change process.

CASE STUDY 2
IMPLEMENTATION

Cherie began this phase by meeting with the members of the change steering committee to clarify the Project Management Tool and review the budget. There was a slight overrun on funds from the last phase, but Cherie believed that the committee would make up that difference by the end of the Implementation phase. Most of the members were excited and optimistic about the prospects of the pilot succeeding.

Bruce and Cherie called all of the employees at a director level or higher position who would remain in their current jobs for an official briefing on the new organizational chart for Northcutt. The chart contained positions, not names. Bruce announced that Human Resources would begin the necessary contacts and interviews with current employees whom they had tabbed to serve in a function under the reorganization. Bruce also noted that, in some cases, even some of the participants in this meeting would be subject to reassignment or layoff and, in other cases, they would remain in their jobs, but with substantial differences in the way they functioned. Needless to say, this meeting caused quite a stir, and word quickly spread among all employees that the change initiative that had been announced months before in the kickoff meeting was now imminent.

In anticipation of this, the next day Bruce called a company-wide meeting at the Kansas City headquarters and gave the essence of the same message he had transmitted to management. Cherie ensured that the communication about the reorganization was extensive. The level of activity was intense. Human Resources, along with a number of subcontracted professionals, held hundreds of meetings with employees to determine placement. Those employees who were laid off were given appropriate options for training, outplacement, and severance. Those employees who would stay in the company, but perform a different job, were given a schedule for relocation and training. Those employees who would stay in their current jobs, but who would perform exceedingly different functions, were given training plans. Not everyone, of course, accepted the change, and there was certainly some instant anger and denial; but for the most part, things proceeded correctly. Some employees actually remarked that they were upset that the western zone was given the chance to try this first!

The change steering committee admittedly was tired, but also excited about seeing the plans they had approved put into action. They were extremely pleased that they had anticipated the potential objections to making the change and had responses ready to provide in practically every case.

The chief interest was in how well the work that employees had performed under "silos" would work under a consolidated arrangement. There was also great anticipation about how the field salesforce would transition into representing all products sold by the company to customers within a geographic territory. Since the product training was all online, the company pulled together the entire field salesforce to a Kansas City hotel for a two-day intensive "Northcutt University," in which cross-functional training about customer preferences took place. Veterans who had sold certain products for years to particular customers transferred knowledge to those who had yet to meet them, and vice versa. The atmosphere was upbeat, yet highly professional, with senior management putting a positive spin on the activities. Bruce gave the keynote speech at the opening banquet in support of the change, encouraged everyone to give it a chance to work, and explained the benefit of the change and how success would be measured.

While Human Resources had already been operating as a consolidated department for some time, the newly aligned marketing, finance, and accounting operations met in Kansas City to get acquainted with each other and work through the nuances of consolidating their work, as per the project plan.

Professionals from Management Information Services were on-site in both of these locations to present and answer questions about changes in the technology used to perform the reorganized functions. As the employees went back to work, MIS was available to debug problems, such as accidentally deleted profiles, missing codes, or transposed products and corresponding marketing information. MIS solved all of these problems quickly by reprogramming the software and reloading it on the intranet as quickly as possible.

In spite of some minor issues and concerns, the western zone and employees at consolidated departments at headquarters rapidly adopted the restructuring and went about their business in ways that customers did not notice anything different. Employees quickly ceased talking about the change and focused on doing their work. Upper management at the company was excited about the prospects for improving business, and everyone on the change steering committee believed that the implementation was successful.

What Could Go Wrong

In the Implementation phase, you need to be ready for potential problems, such as these:

Problem: Users may find the systems are difficult to use and the change steering committee may underestimate the level of support required during the pilot.

Solution: This is obviously a problem that requires assistance from supervisors and staff in the organization. If the change steering committee sees that it has underestimated the amount of support required for the pilot, it should regroup prior to full implementation. One possibility is to select some competent users from the pilot to serve as mentors and coaches for others during the full implementation. Another possibility is to hire external contractors to provide additional support, although this may negatively impact the budget.

Problem: The change steering committee decides that two pilots are necessary due to logistical concerns.

Solution: There are a variety of reasons that the change steering committee could make this determination, not the least of which is to ensure that the organization "gets it right" prior to full implementation. One solution is to extend the timeline for the initiative to allow for some corrections between the first and second pilot runs. Interestingly, if the change steering committee proposes a system for the change initiative that does not work in a pilot, what confidence would the members have that it would work under conditions of full implementation?

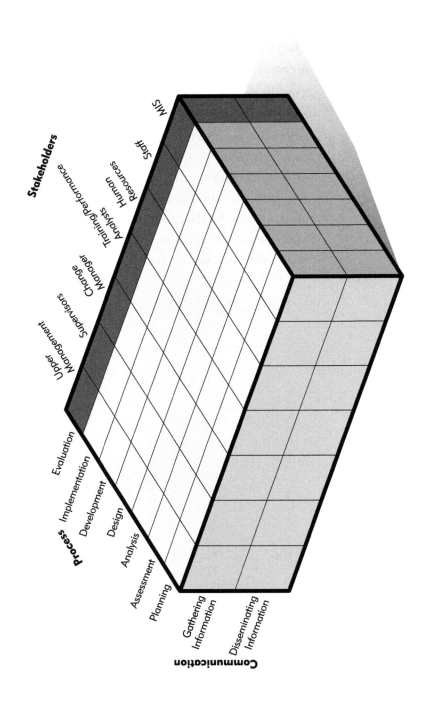

12

Evaluation

THIS PHASE MEASURES the effectiveness of the change, both short-term and long-term. This chapter explains how to evaluate a change initiative. Remember that Evaluation actually begins during the Design phase with the formation of objectives and that in previous chapters we discussed the strategies for evaluating the initiative. This is where we provide the specific tools and techniques. An evaluation cannot be accomplished in a short period of time. It takes time to see the results of change.

Inputs

The input to this phase is a fully implemented initiative.

Outputs

The output of this phase is an Evaluation of the results of the project.

Responsibilities/Activities

Table 12.1 lists each stakeholder's responsibilities during the Evaluation phase.

Table 12.1. Responsibilities During Evaluation.

Evaluation

Upper Management

- Conduct company celebratory meeting
- Commend the project team and the groups that implemented the change publicly

Supervisors

- Manage the new program

Change Manager

- Coordinate completing the Project Management Tool
- Coordinate evaluation of the project
- Present the evaluation results to upper management and the entire company
- Continue to monitor the progress of the change on an ongoing basis, possibly as functional operational manager

Training/Performance Analysts

- Teach Evaluation phase
- Train observers and interviewers
- Develop and validate evaluation instruments
- Conduct return-on-investment (ROI) study
- Analyze Evaluation data
- Write Evaluation Report
- Periodically monitor the program
- Coordinate training of new employees as needed who will be trained by the on-the-job trainers
- Monitor long-term organizational performance

Human Resources

- Monitor career progression development plans and attrition

Staff

- Train department employees on an ongoing basis
- Conduct observations
- Assist training department to complete ROI study

Management Information Services

- Maintain systems

Shared Responsibilities

- Support company celebratory meeting

Upper Management

Upper management should publicly commend the change steering committee for its efforts and provide some tangible reward for their efforts. The reward should be based on the level of success of the project. One example is a bonus once the project is fully implemented and profit sharing for the steering committee and all the groups that have been impacted by the change after the first full year of implementation. Upper management should sponsor an upbeat company-wide celebratory meeting and announce some of the important results.

Supervisors

Supervisors from the division where the new program is implemented need to be sure that employees are using the systems and procedures in accordance with their design. This is an ongoing task as long as the organization continues to use the initiative.

Change Manager

The change manager must coordinate the evaluation and assist in preparation and presentation of the results to upper management. The change manager should also monitor the change on an ongoing basis, perhaps as the functional operations manager over the departments affected by the change.

Note: A functional operations manager might be a position that was determined during the Analysis phase as being required to manage the business. The position is "functional" because it might require the manager to monitor and coordinate functions in several departments. Another result might have been an operational restructuring to establish a new department. This is an example of how a change in one area of the company might have a ripple effect on other parts of the organization.

Training/Performance Analysts

Training conducts the evaluation once the change is fully implemented, measuring the desired performance against the actual performance and working with the financial analyst to complete the ROI study. Together, they gather and interpret the data and write the final Evaluation Report.

Remember that the best initiative in the world will not change anything if it is not used properly. Therefore, the training professionals' jobs do not end at the time the final report is made available. Training and performance analysts must be assigned to periodically monitor the long-term performance of the initiative to be certain that it continues to perform as required. They need to provide feedback to various departments and divisions about their performance on the new system and request that their supervisors make corrections if performance begins to drop off.

Note: An initiative will initially show an increase in performance because everyone is concentrating on it and it is receiving a lot of attention. However, if not monitored and reinforced, performance may begin to decline. The reason for this decline is that former habits and ways of performing work may creep back in and familiar procedures will begin to be used again. However, under new conditions, doing work in the old way can impede work being performed effectively and efficiently throughout the company. Gains from the change will be lost if these issues are not immediately addressed. Less monitoring will be required once all of the processes for the change have been used for a long period of time. Figure 12.1 demonstrates the productivity curve and where interventions must be initiated.

Figure 12.1. Productivity Curve.

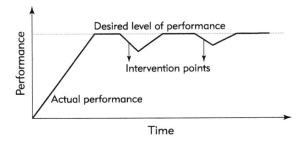

In addition, these professionals should coordinate training on the new system for all new employees using the on-the-job trainers for the staff members from the original change steering committee. Training should never be left to supervisors or simply left to mentoring by experienced employees. Each new employee who will be using the system needs to receive the information directly and accurately, without benefit of the shortcuts that the more experienced employees have found. New employees will certainly obtain "helpful hints" from fellow employees, but they should receive the official version first and be able to decide whether the shortcuts are really beneficial to them. The periodic monitoring of the program will help ensure that no shortcuts creep in that are detrimental to the program.

Training and performance analysts are responsible for creating the observation instruments. (We cover creating observation instruments later in this chapter.) You should use supervisors, staff members, and other expert performers to develop the observation criteria. These three groups should come to consensus on the observable criteria. Achieving consensus assures that the content of the observation form is accurate. This is known as content validity. The focus group technique covered in this chapter is a good method to achieve the required content validity. Training and performance analysts must also train observers who will be making site visits and validating the issues identified during Analysis. The goal is to be certain that all observers rate the same criteria in the same way.

Human Resources

Human Resources has the ongoing responsibility of monitoring the career progression and attrition plans for employees. They must replace employees who are promoted or who leave.

Staff

The staff committee members will conduct interviews and make observations during the Evaluation phase and provide the ongoing training of new employees on the system, with the assistance of the training and performance analysts. In addition, they should conduct "train-the-trainer" classes for the staff members from the affected groups to ensure a constant supply of highly skilled instructors on the new system.

The financial analyst will assist training/performance analysts and the change manager in conducting the ROI study.

Management Information Services

If the initiative involves a physical system, technical staff members in MIS must maintain it and keep it operational, much as they did during the pilot test, but now for the long term.

Shared Responsibilities

All committee members must support the ongoing change, doing their part to make adjustments to the system as needed when recommended by the training and performance analysts.

All steering committee members should attend the company celebration meeting and have the opportunity to state how they feel the new initiative will help the organization and give testimonials to support any results obtained from the summative evaluation.

Data Analysis

Plan your evaluation thoroughly before you run it. Some things are recoverable because they are in the data and you only need to analyze them in a different way, but some things might not be recoverable unless you run the entire evaluation project again—costing time, money, and a delay in obtaining the final results.

You need a statistical analyst on the change steering committee who is experienced in data-gathering techniques and data analysis. After interpretation of the statistical findings, anyone with good problem-solving skills can determine what the data mean.

There are four activities required in data collection and analysis:

1. Set up the database files in the statistical package for entering the data.

2. Collect and run the data.

3. Interpret the data.

4. Document your findings in the Evaluation Report.

Use any of the statistical packages available to set up the database to capture information or transfer information from other sources. There are numerous packages on the market for this purpose.

Capture data using the measurement instruments developed in this phase, which are based on the objectives formulated during the Design phase. Capture as many responses as possible. Interpret the data against the goals for the project and determine whether the results match the findings. If the goals match the results, you might choose to do one of the following:

- Do a full-scale implementation of the solution and continue to collect data for consistent results;

- Do a full-scale implementation and discontinue collecting data; or

- Do a full-scale implementation and wait for a certain period of time, then conduct another evaluation.

If the results do not match the goals, you might decide to take one of the following steps:

- Revise the initiative;

- Revise the measurement instruments;

- Rerun the study with revisions;

- Choose another representative sample and rerun the evaluation; or

- Discard the initiative.

Return on Investment

You will want to conduct a return-on-investment (ROI) analysis after you have implemented the change initiative. The results indicate the number of dollars returned for each dollar spent on the change initiative.

The benefit of the change is determined by the objectives you established during the Design phase. There you found from upper management what they required as a return and weighted that against the cost of the change. It may have been increased profit, cost avoidance, or whatever. The measurement is called the cost/benefit analysis (CBA). The formula for calculating CBA is (Lee & Owens, 2000):

Total Desired $ Benefit ÷ Total Anticipated $ Cost = Cost/Benefit

For example, if the total desired benefit during CBA was $10,000,000 after the first year of implementation and the anticipated cost was $1,000,000, the CBA ratio would be 10:1 (for every dollar spent, ten dollars would be returned).

The ROI formula is:

ROI = Net Program Benefits/Program Costs × 100

Net program benefits are the benefit minus the cost = $10,000,000 − $1,000,000 = $9,000,000

For the above example, $9,000,000 in profit realized after the first year of implementation, divided by the $1,000,000 spent on the project multiplied by 100 to account for the percentage would yield a 900 percent return.

Net profit is a different calculation than ROI. Net profit would be:

Gross $ Profit − $ Cost for Implementation = $ Net Profit

In this case, $10,000,000 − $1,000,000 = $9,000,000.

As another example, if the company's net profit before the change was $70,000,000, the percentage of increased profit would be:

$70,000,000 ÷ $9,000,000 = 7.8% Increased Profit

You can use Exhibit 12.1 to help you determine all the costs associated with CBA, ROI, gross profit, and net profit calculations. Direct costs are those costs that are charged against the project. Indirect costs are those costs that the company would incur in addition to the direct costs of the project. Depending on the way a company calculates direct and indirect costs, certain categories in the indirect cost categories may move to direct costs. For example, a company may include personnel salaries and benefits as direct charges to the project. The company might also charge the salaries and benefits of employees who must do the work of those on the steering committee against the cost of the project. Or a company may not charge the

Exhibit 12.1. Cost Calculation Template.

Type of Cost	Planning	Assessment	Analysis	Design	Development	Implementation	Evaluation
Direct							
Personnel							
Equipment							
Supplies							
Facilities							
Services							
Travel							
Total Direct Costs							
Indirect							
Personnel							
Facilities							
Benefits							
Total Indirect Costs							
Total Costs							

cost of equipment against the project, such as the computers the committee members will use while working on the project, if they are the same computers that would be used in performing their regular jobs. Those costs not charged as either direct or indirect costs are considered to be "sunk costs." In other words, a company would incur them regardless of whether or not it was undertaking the change. Your financial analyst will know what your company typically charges against projects.

Constructing Instruments

Tests, questionnaires, surveys, and observation instruments must all be developed based on the purpose of the evaluation. All measurement instruments must attain the degree of validity, as determined by the training/performance analysts, required to return information containing any degree of certainty about the effectiveness of the change (Lee & Owens, 2000). The required degrees of validity from data collected during the pilot test or through any forms of validity are discussed by Shrock, Coscarelli & Eyres (2000).

Interview instruments, as with questionnaires and surveys, must attain a certain degree of content validity to be useful. There are two ways to measure validity: quantitative and qualitative. Qualitative measures, although they use data, require more professional judgment; quantitative measures rely more heavily on standardized methods of interpreting statistics—although some will argue that there is judgment involved in the interpretation, with which we agree.

The key is knowing which statistical tests to use and how to interpret the data you receive. The statistical analyst on the project team will know how to interpret the data. However, here are some common statistical measures of validity with an explanation of when and how to use them.

Frequency Counts

Frequency counts are a quantitative measure but require judgment to determine their benefit. Frequencies are easy to generate even if you don't use a statistical package. Just count the number of responses based on some standard (for example, correct/incorrect). However, a statistical package generates the data much faster, especially for large numbers of cases. Judgment is involved in the setting of the frequency level for success or failure.

Difficulty Index

You can also look at the level of difficulty for a task. For example, when making observations, you must determine how long it takes all those being observed to complete the task. The steering committee must determine what is an acceptable amount of time they will allow to complete the task. They could decide that the time it takes the person who completed it the fastest would be the acceptable time or the person who completed it the slowest would be the baseline. Another way to calculate this would be to add all the times from all those observed and derive an average. The average is the 50th percentile. But maybe the committee would decide that the performance must be at the 75th percentile to be acceptable. They would then choose that time. The decision would depend on those elements identified in issue analysis and prioritization during Analysis.

Example: Here are the times in minutes for five exemplary performers completing a manual task: 10, 7, 5, 6, 5. The total time would be 33 minutes. If the committee chose the most time it took someone to perform the task as the criterion, they would choose 10 minutes. If they chose the least amount of time, that would be 5 minutes. If they chose the average time, it would be 6.6 minutes. If they chose the 75th percentile, that would be 8.3 minutes.

Item Analysis

Item analysis determines whether the individual performance items and the overall evaluation instrument are valid. Item analysis establishes validity through the determination that those who performed best overall also performed correctly on a particular item. To perform an item analysis you must have two independent variables that can be compared in some way to make the determination about how good your items are.

Correlation

Correlations establish the relationship between two variables. The result is a number between -1.0 and $+1.0$. Numbers closer to $+1.0$ indicate a high positive correlation. Numbers closer to -1.0 indicate a high negative correlation. The higher the positive correlation, the better the item. But what about questions that receive 0.00? You must then use the difficulty index to determine whether to include or exclude the item from your assessment instrument. Consider the time it takes for an employee to complete a certain activity. If there is a high positive correlation between the time taken to complete and the correctness, then you would use that person's procedure to complete the activity. If there were no correlation or a high negative correlation, you would not count that person's time to complete the task among the calculations of the others observed.

Tests of Significance

Tests of significance are used when you want to determine whether the results you obtain from your sample group are typical of the total population from which the random sample was drawn. To do this, begin by determining whether you will administer measures before and/or after implementing the change. If both before and after, you should use the same instrument both times.

If you make an observation where employees have multiple chances to successfully complete the task, you can perform a frequency count to determine how many attempts were required for most of them to accomplish the task. If the number is low, that observation item is valid. If there are some tasks that it takes more tries to accomplish, you had better check that item; the task should probably not be included in the list of tasks that are required for the job.

Evaluation Plan and Report

The Evaluation Plan outlines how the project will be evaluated. Sections I and II of the plan is completed during Design and Sections III, IV, and V are completed after the project is implemented. The completed Evaluation Plan then becomes the Evaluation Report.

The Evaluation Report consists of five sections:

1. Executive summary

2. Background information

3. Findings

4. Conclusions and recommendations

5. Appendices

Exhibit 12.2 is an example of an Evaluation Plan and Report. It can be used as a template; for each section, there is a description of its purpose and the type of information that should be included.

Exhibit 12.2. Evaluation Plan and Report.

Section I—Executive Summary

This section is a brief overview of the entire report, explaining the basis for the evaluation and the significant conclusions and recommendations. *(You may consider using headings parallel to the general report—Sections II, III, IV, and V—to maintain uniformity):*

-
-
-

Section II—Background Information

Introduction: This section includes a general description of the evaluation and the reasons for conducting the evaluation.

Purpose: The purpose of the evaluation is to *(state the purpose of the evaluation, what you are measuring and why).*

For this project, the evaluation focused on the following questions:

-
-
-

(Continued)

Exhibit 12.2. Evaluation Plan and Report. (Continued)

Roles and Responsibilities: The following lists the roles and responsibilities of the steering committee and others that participated in this project.

Name	Role	Responsibility
	Change Manager	
	Supervisors	
	Training/Performance Analysts	
	Human Resources	
	MIS	
	Staff Members	

Data-Collection Methods: The change manager and project team members perform the evaluation. *(Describe the role of committee members.)*

The following paragraphs describe the methods and instruments used to collect the evaluation data. *(Briefly describe the process/tools used to collect, analyze, report, and preserve the evaluation data.)*

Section III—Findings
This section summarizes the findings of the evaluation.

Section IV—Conclusions and Recommendations
This section reports the interpretation of the findings.

Section V—Appendices
This section contains the supporting data from the analysis.

CASE STUDY 1
EVALUATION

After the initial three departments worked on the system and as the bugs and obstacles worked themselves out, the committee and upper management decided that the change initiative was ready for full-scale implementation using all major areas of the company. The next six areas that joined the original three were Sales, Buyers, Graphic Arts, New Product Development, Corporate Communications, and Legal. More than two hundred users were involved as this phase rolled out. Not only were employee attitudes and productivity under scrutiny, but there was also attention to removing final bugs as well.

Senior management took a totally "hands-off" stance during the full-scale rollout. They had complete confidence that the change steering committee and all the groups throughout the organization had done their jobs well. Because of the expense and investment in the initiative to date, they were anxious to see what kinds of results would be realized. In spite of this, they managed to use restraint and not interfere with any of the process.

Supervisors in these six departments met with Jess and others from the committee, who urged them to support their employees as much as possible during the transition time. They were told to expect questions, frustrations, and mistakes and to show extra patience. They were also introduced to several members of the MIS technical team and several training/performance analysts who were very involved during the recently completed pilot and could help out with any difficulties. On-the-job training consisting of quick refresher courses and direct assistance were among the top priorities for training/performance analysts.

By the time the pilot test was over, MIS had most of the technical problems worked out and proceeded to make the changes in all company computers. Data from the pilot test revealed a reduction in processing time, response time, error rates, research time, printing time, and distribution costs. Productivity increased by 75 percent using the new system, and those who participated in the pilot enjoyed the new ease with which they could complete their work. With the increased productivity, the company would realize its desired return on its investment within three years.

Here is an example of one of the successes after implementing SAP. Blumroth spends a large amount of money in marketing funds each year on consumer-redeemable coupons, which are part of a negotiated arrangement with product manufacturers. The coupons entitle users to discount purchases, 2-for-1 offers, or buy one–get one free opportunities. Consumers obtain these coupons in a variety of ways, including newspapers, direct mail, Internet sites, cash register receipts, and on products in an "instantly redeemable" style. When consumers use these coupons at Blumroth, the store collects them and returns them to the manufacturer for payment. In order to track the source and authenticity of these payments, the company required authorization signatures from no fewer than seven different employees at a variety of levels, representing four different departments. This process ultimately slowed the release of the check to a retail store, which waited more than sixty days before receiving reimbursement for the coupons. This delay especially irritated franchisees. Implementing SAP cut the number of signatures from seven to three, the number of departments involved from four to two, and the reimbursement time from more than two months to less than twenty days.

Word spread quickly about the satisfaction people were experiencing using the new system. The CEO presided over one final meeting to announce the good news to the entire organization and launch the change company-wide. He also honored the change steering committee with a very substantial bonus.

Eighteen months after the full-scale implementation, the final step was to complete the Evaluation Plan and Report. In preparation for this, professionals from finance worked with change steering committee members to conduct a return-on-investment (ROI) study to determine the real financial costs and benefits to the company for implementing SAP. As with any ROI endeavor, gathering and analyzing data was a time-consuming task, but the outcomes were very favorable, with Blumroth obtaining a positive ROI of 69.33. When this outcome was benchmarked against other similar-size companies that had implemented SAP, the results put Blumroth in the top 25 percent, which was a very satisfying result for Jess and the entire upper management team.

After the change steering committee made two revisions of the Evaluation Plan and Report, Jess submitted it to upper management, who were obviously quite pleased with the outcome. The move to SAP was a successful change initiative, organized and executed extremely well.

CASE STUDY 2
EVALUATION

The change steering committee had always worked with the "end in mind." One of the reasons that they and senior management had paid such close attention to the objectives was so that they could use them to determine the success and failure of the initiative. Therefore, when the committee entered the Evaluation phase, they focused on issues that they actually had considered long before.

The entire committee worked to involve managers at all levels to provide data in order that they could evaluate their objectives from the pilot. Simultaneously, Hugh and some finance professionals helped pull together data for the budget and ROI analysis.

The committee also initiated focus group meetings among the affected departments to discuss what the employees felt about the change now that Northcutt had implemented it, what problems they had encountered, and what they believed should take place in the near future.

In all cases, the initiative was given a green light. The pilot results were extremely positive, and the feeling was that the company was wasting time and resources by not putting the initiative into a full rollout. Bruce announced this would be the case just four days after receiving a complete pilot report.

The communication in the company in this phase emphasized the acclimating nature of the change within Northcutt. Senior management urged all managers to meet with their employees, provide them "long leashes" to learn and implement the new tasks, and otherwise support them as much as possible. Everyone was assured that there would be mistakes, frustrations, and questions. All of these were anticipated and realized.

The biggest surprise to everyone was how few technical problems the company encountered during the implementation of the change. Bruce and Cherie were quick to commend MIS professionals on the superb way that they had anticipated most of the technical problems and had been thoroughly prepared to solve any issues that arose.

Human Resources professionals continued to monitor the outplacement contracts and also continued to counsel employees who had agreed to work under the reorganization and to overcome difficulties by coordinating with the training/performance analysis department.

Marv was able to release many of the external training firms from their contracts as more employees became proficient in the skills required for their jobs, and as more of the training transferred to the company's own training department.

At their final meeting, Cherie told the change steering committee that she was pleased by how senior management had supported their work without interfering or trying to unduly influence any process. She said that the reason for this was that the committee had never acted irresponsibly and always seemed to operate in the best interests of the company.

The Evaluation Plan and Report consisted of a customer satisfaction survey conducted nine months into the initiative and an employee satisfaction survey administered at the eleven-month point. Both of these measures showed a high degree of satisfaction with the organizational change. Productivity measures showed an increase of 15 percent within six months and 22 percent within one year. The company showed anticipated profit levels within eighteen months and actually exceeded its return on investment within three years. The company achieved its goal of becoming number 1 or number 2 in all product lines.

Cherie was named vice president of the new organization to serve as the functional operational manager to oversee the change on an ongoing basis.

Senior managers wanted to celebrate the outstanding work that Cherie and her steering committee had performed over all those months. A month after Implementation they took the entire committee and their significant others to a lunch at a nice steakhouse in Kansas City. The only requirement of the group was that they could discuss work for a total of fifteen minutes and, after that, have fun. They held an awards ceremony for the steering committee and presented trophies. All ancillary committee members and the groups that implemented the change were treated to a lunch at headquarters in Kansas City and received certificates. Everyone who implemented the change was guaranteed a bonus at the end of the first year of the project based on the increased profit from the change.

What Could Go Wrong

The following are some potential problems that you may encounter in the Evaluation phase:

Problem: Unanticipated costs during the previous phases may create cost overruns that will make the project fall short of the desired ROI.

Solution: The change manager may have to request permission from upper management to make a projection of more than one year to achieve the desired rate of return.

Problem: Results of the pilot may not yield projections that will reach the desired ROI.

Solution: The change steering committee has a variety of options available, and the members should discuss the potential benefits or consequences carefully before proceeding. One is to convince upper management to accept the lower ROI. Another is to alter or eliminate some element in the "cost" category to reduce expenses. A third option is to extend the timeframe for the organization to reach the desired ROI. Still another, that we cannot ignore, is to abandon the initiative.

Problem: Upper management and change steering committee members may be unfamiliar with statistical techniques and terminology, thus necessitating a choice for the Evaluation Plan and Report between (1) writing a highly basic and very thorough explanation or (2) providing the results only and going forward.

Solution: This is a determination that must be made depending on the intended audience for the report. The real question is how much interest or concern the reader(s) will have for the background to the report that produces the results. The change manager could query representatives of the different audiences and then make a determination based on their interests and needs.

Having reached the conclusion of the Evaluation phase, you have completed the required steps for organizing a change initiative. Our attention now turns to two aspects of communication: gathering information and disseminating information, which have an impact for practically every phase in the process you have just completed.

Unit 4

Communication

13

Gathering Information

COMMUNICATION IS THE CORNERSTONE for a successful change initiative. By definition, if the initiative is to be inclusive, every participant in the process communicates by gathering and disseminating information. Chapters 13 and 14 discuss the factors and skills involved with both of these aspects of communication. Here we place most of our emphasis on fact-finding skills you can use to gather information. Note that you can use these skills during any phase of the change initiative. We then apply these skills to several methods for gathering information, which include conducting interviews and holding focus groups.

Quality and Quantity of Information During Change

There are always two ways that we can evaluate information—quantity and quality. The satisfaction that participants in a change initiative express with the communication almost always revolves around these two issues. When an individual does not have enough information, he or she cannot make a proper decision. This is a condition of underload. When an individual receives more information than he or she can reasonably process, he or she is likely to either miss important data, or devote an inordinate amount of time to sorting through it, thus affecting other tasks or responsibilities. This is a condition of overload. When an individual has the proper amount of information, but it is not useful, interpretable, or relevant, his or her participation in the change process is affected negatively.

These quantity and quality issues define the way that everyone gathers and disseminates information during routine times, as well as in the midst of a change initiative. How much and what kind of information do you need to receive in order to maintain productivity during change? How much and what kind of information do you need to provide in order to maintain productivity during change? You will find many of the tactics that we refer to in this section very helpful to monitor quantity and quality as you gather information during a change initiative.

Communication in a Change Context

One of the most difficult, but important issues to clarify is to ensure that we fully understand what we mean by communication and why it is important to increase proficiency in these skills. You would have difficulty finding anyone who does not profess to both understanding communication and doing it very well. You would also have difficulty finding anyone who could not name at least one colleague or acquaintance who is less than proficient at some aspect of communication.

Communication involves three hierarchical levels: (1) one person prepares and sends information; (2) another person receives and interprets that information; and then, (3) that person acts on the information (see Figure 13.1). The process may break down in any of these steps. An individual may prepare information and choose not to transmit it. Another person may never open an e-mail or just miss a meeting. Still another person "hears" the message another person sends, but communication actually ends with the sound waves hitting the eardrums, and the receiver does not actually "listen."

Figure 13.1. Levels of Communication in Change.

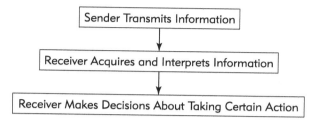

Another person listens to a message that a sender intends to be facetious or sarcastic, but processes it seriously. Finally, another person receives and interprets the message correctly, but simply does not want to take the suggested action. Unfortunately, you will likely encounter problems with all three of these levels as you work in a change initiative in most organizations.

For our purpose in these chapters, we want to restrict our look at communication in two ways. First, communication is goal-oriented. Therefore, we are only interested in communication that has a purpose and that we can evaluate the results of, in order to label it successful or unsuccessful. Second, communication is verbal. We are only interested in the words, whether oral or written, rather than in non-verbal elements such as volume, pacing, tone, gestures, or eye contact. In saying this, we want to acknowledge the existence and importance of messages that are unintentional and that another person receives meaning from, as well as the power of non-verbal factors in communication. These are simply parameters that we want to place on our discussion, since this book specifically focuses on change, rather than generally on communication, and since gathering and disseminating information appropriately is integral to our change model.

Fact-Finding

Fact-finding is the most frequently used way that participants in an organization gather information they wish to share with others for a change initiative. Fact-finding is comprised of several important communication skills that employees must master throughout the process as they meet with each other and with clients, suppliers, vendors, or customers.

When employees fact-find correctly, they are able to analyze or diagnose an issue first, then take or suggest action steps second. With fact-finding, employees can build and enhance meaningful business relationships and partnerships with others. They will be more successful in achieving their intended outcomes. They will take a solutions orientation toward a change initiative as they interact with others.

If you ever diagnose before you fact-find, you fall into the trap of "ready-fire-aim." You propose a solution in search of a problem or issue. Fact-finding allows you to follow the sequence "ready-aim-fire," which means that you first discover the nature of a problem or issue, if any exists, then offer a means to solve the problem.

Not surprisingly, most people accomplish fact-finding through asking others a series of questions. However, there are also other ways to fact-find, including making observations and examining records, data, or correspondence. Regardless of the method that you use, fact-finding is the first step in diagnosis. In every part of your life, whether you want to refer to car repair, a visit to a physician, or a machine that malfunctions, the professional you interact with asks you a series of questions in order to uncover the relevant problem, issue, or cause. You would probably walk out of a medical doctor's office who opens the door, takes one look at you from head to toe, and diagnoses you as having appendicitis, then calls for an ambulance to rush you to a hospital for surgery. Or how long would you stay at an automobile repair shop where the technician kicks your tire and declares that you need an engine overhaul. Throughout all phases of the change process, you will find an important need for diagnosis through asking proper fact-finding questions.

To gather information well, you need to view fact-finding as a process of inquiry and discovery, not advocacy. You will reach poor conclusions if you engage in fact-finding to build a case, rather than to discover whether there is a case to build.

Additionally, the focus of your questions should not be on you, but on the person you interact with. In today's busy work environment, with all the pressures that everyone faces, you are very fortunate to obtain even five minutes' time with someone. You will find that people will give you much more time, and demonstrate much more interest, when they perceive that they will receive at least a minimal return on their investment.

One of the key strategies that you can use to elicit time and cooperation from another person is to explain the purpose and how you or others will use the information you gather. In most cases, you should think about a mutual gain that the individual could accrue from spending time with you. For example, will the answers he or she gives you ultimately provide ways to make changes that produce more meaningful, more efficient, less pressured, or more rewarding work? Of course, you cannot promise any of these outcomes, but when the other person is aware that his or her answers may contribute to something important, you can expect more cooperation, enthusiasm, and time. In addition, your time together can enhance the relationship that exists between the two of you.

Finally, fact-finding always has a purpose. It is never an end to itself. With the expectation of building relationships by showing an interest in someone, you want to fact-find in order to accomplish a goal that is important to the success of the change initiative. Any of the following are reasons to fact-find effectively:

- Gathering information;

- Persuading, convincing, or selling;

- Solving problems;

- Making decisions; or

- Taking appropriate action.

Steps in Fact-Finding

Fact-finding involves four basic steps:

1. Make the right observations in advance of asking questions.

2. From these observations, ask your focus person the right questions.

3. Listen to the answers you receive, and decide whether you need to probe for more information or clarification.

4. Use the answers in a way that achieves your objective.

First, you need to make the right observations in advance of asking questions. Your observations about people and processes, along with any examination you might do with correspondence, files, or records, should yield some interesting areas for later questions and discussion.

For example, one convenience store owner had never thought about advertising products and services at the outside gasoline pumps until a salesperson told her that he had filled up the car, watched as twenty-seven other cars came and went in fifteen minutes, and saw only two people walk into the store. He asked, "Are you interested in finding ways to bring more than two out of twenty-seven customers into your store to spend money?" Of course the owner was.

Second, from these observations, you need to ask the right questions, whether via a meeting, phone call, or e-mail. What are the questions that relate to your objective in gathering information? What are the potential answers to your question? More importantly, what do you plan to do with the answers you receive?

The third step is to decide whether you need to probe for more information or clarification. All too often we ask the first question, receive an answer, and move on, when in fact, we have not received the quantity or quality of information we really need.

The fourth step is to use the answers in a way that achieves your objective. Perhaps you summarize these answers in a meeting. You may wish to tabulate the variety of answers you receive, such as you might for a survey. You may also use an answer you receive to confront or challenge someone who disagrees with you, to provide guidance on areas of philosophical disagreement, or to give direction to the change initiative.

In summary, in order to be successful during fact-finding, try to do these things:

1. Keep an open-mind while you engage in the process. Avoid having any expectations or predispositions that could bias what you see or hear. Listen to the message before you act on it by summarizing, judging, or criticizing an answer in your mind.

2. Use your eyes as well as your mouth. Often some of the best sources of information are not what someone tells you in response to a question, but rather what you can see for yourself. If an employee tells you, "I am never late," but you observe him frequently arriving at work ten to fifteen minutes after the official beginning of the work day, what would you believe?

3. Try not to become so focused on asking your next question that you forget to listen to the person you are talking with. The ultimate value of fact-finding is in the answers you receive, not in the questions you ask.

Maximizing the Value of Fact-Finding

We have seen several instances over the years where fact-finding has not achieved its purpose. Here are some principles you can use to minimize the chances of this happening to you during a change initiative.

First, stay in the questioning process long enough to gain a full understanding of the other person's position. Many people receive an answer to a question and then, feeling satisfied, simply move forward. This can be a significant barrier to the process. After hearing a factual answer, you can also ask for the person's feelings or attitudes.

For example, during a one-on-one meeting, a highly innovative employee asked a manager, "How are we doing on our budget in the first six months of the year?" The manager replied, "We are ahead by 10 percent." The employee went on to another topic, rather than asking questions such as these, which would likely have elicited additional information:

- *"Are you satisfied with that?"*

- *"Do you think that's good?"*

- *"Do you have any problem with that?"*

- *"Are there additional opportunities for us to . . . ?"*

- *"Is there still a need to . . . ?"*

Second, avoid solving the other person's problem or issue while fact-finding. Remember that you are wearing a fact-finding cap, not a solutions cap nor a selling cap. Your purpose is to obtain information about an issue or problem, not to solve the issue or problem. This is easier said than done. In many cases, because we either know or can anticipate how someone may answer a question, or because the other person has motivated us to do so, we can easily slip into a solution-providing mode. Whenever this happens, you will lose your focus on gathering information. This does not mean that you should not ask, "What would you do?" or "What do you think the real issue is?" Those questions also seek to gather information.

Third, use a variety of communication tactics while fact-finding. We describe different methods that you can use to gather information from another person in the Communication Tactics section of this chapter. We want to caution you not to fall into a rut of using your favorites or to heavily rely on one that has worked well for you.

For example, you may have used the tactic entitled "restatement" that we introduce below. Restatements are also labeled "mirror" or "reflective" questions, and they simply use the other person's words, offered with an upward inflection, which stimulates him or her to further develop or clarify an answer. They are some of the most popular tactics for gathering information that we have available. Suppose that you use this tactic during fact-finding with a person once, twice, three times, and then a fourth. Would you be surprised if she said, "Excuse me, but are you hard of hearing?" She may also become irritable, replying with "That's what I said!" Be careful not to go to the well too many times with the same tactic. People who are the best at fact-finding are also the best at mixing the various tactics for gathering information.

Communication Tactics to Gather Information

Following are descriptions and examples of five communication tactics that you can use to fact-find and gather information. These five tactics are general leads, probes, pauses, restatements, and interpretations.

General Leads

General leads are used to introduce or change topics. They are "stock" questions used to introduce a variety of topics. They are the starting point in a conversation or a transition point to a new topic. General leads are open-ended questions that give the person you are talking with room to discuss any aspect of the situation. Begin general lead questions with words that allow the other person to open up and talk. For example:

- "*How* do you determine what is appropriate for a customer?"

- "*How* do the different geographic regions vary in sales of our product?"

- "Please *tell me* how you worked through some difficult situations."
- "*Tell me* about the different options that you have available."
- "Please *describe* the ways you receive incorrect information."
- "*Describe* the training you give to a new employee."
- "*Explain* what our competition does differently."
- "*Explain* what your new plans are for the coming year."

Probes

By definition, a probing question follows an answer you receive from a general lead. You decide to ask a follow-up question in order to clarify an answer, to obtain more information, or simply to show interest in the other person. We often discount this third reason. Yet, if you believe that one of the purposes of fact-finding is to enhance relationships, then probing for the purpose of showing interest is not to be ignored. This is the same skill, often called "small talk," that we use at parties, church, picnics, or other social endeavors when we introduce ourselves and get to know others.

Probes can be either open-ended or closed-ended. Open probes allow the other person the opportunity to define the question and elaborate on the previous answer through his or her eyes. Probes begin with the same terms as general leads:

- "*How* did that happen?"
- "*Describe* the steps you took when you went there."
- "*Tell me* the most enjoyable part."
- "*Explain* the circumstances in the order in which they occurred."

There are occasions that require specific information from the person you are talking with. These are the times to use closed probes. The closed probe limits the range of the person's response to a "yes" or "no," to a choice among alternatives that you supply, or to a specific piece of information that you want to know. Closed probes begin with:

- "*Do* you believe that the employees could improve?"
- "*Does* senior management take the same perspective that you do?"

- "*Is* there any chance the demand for our products will diminish?"

- "*Are* there any courses that your people have not yet taken?"

- "*Which* diversity initiatives have made the biggest impact here?"

- "*What* do you think the customer really wanted?"

- "*When* did you receive the first signal that there would be trouble?"

Here are the keys to successful probing. First, select a word from the person's previous response that is ambiguous, vague, or needs clarification. Be careful not to assume shared meaning with the person that you are talking with. "What do you mean by. . . ?" is an excellent probing question that ensures that both of you are on the same page. Look at the list of terms below and ask yourself whether or not they would mean the same thing to different people.

- Clutter

- Kids

- Too much

- Too high

- Too slow

- Too expensive

- Steady

- Outstanding

- High-quality

- Good price

- Too long

- Out-of-date

Second, do not sell or solve. Remember that you are learning about an issue and wearing an information cap. Third, picture the general lead as being at the top of a funnel. Your purpose is to ask questions and stay with the topic, narrowing down the focus as you work with the other person.

Here are some examples of general leads, answers, and accompanying open (O) or closed (C) probes:

Lead: "Tell me about your most successful employee."

Answer: "I never have to ask her to do anything. She always seems to anticipate exactly what we need to do in every situation."

Probe: (O) "Please describe one of those recent situations to me."

Lead: "How do you decide how much to spend for training?"

Answer: "I just called some of my friends in other companies and asked them what they spent; then I set my own limits here."

Probe: (C) "What was the range that their spending covered?"

Lead: "Describe the procedures you use for selecting what suppliers or contractors to use."

Answer: "We look at five different criteria. It's not a snap decision by any means."

Probe: (O) "Tell me about those criteria."

Lead: "Please tell me about your employee demographics."

Answer: "We have all kinds of people here. All ages, races, educational background, social strata, rich, poor—if it exists, we've got it."

Probe: (C) "How many college-educated employees work here?"

Lead: "Tell me about a typical phone call that causes you difficulty."

Answer: "First, they are always uninformed. Second, they really aren't ready to talk to me, or even to ask questions. It seems like I have to talk to them to get them ready to talk to me. Third, they are horribly indecisive and can't make a decision."

Probe: (O) "Describe the most frustrating call you have received this week."

Lead: "How do you respond when you receive a request from an employee to telecommute or work some out of the home?"

Answer: "Our human resources department usually makes the decision about those kinds of requests. Occasionally, they ask for suggestions from people like me."

Probe: (C) "What kinds of suggestions have you given in the past?"

Lead: "Describe your outlook on your business for the next year."

Answer: "Not too good. I think the economy is getting people to rethink their priorities and how they will spend their money. Our challenge is to stay ahead of the curve and anticipate our customers' needs so that we have something to fill them with before they actually take their business elsewhere."

Probe: (O) "Tell me how you think we got into this situation."

Lead: "How did you come to the decision to purchase the insurance for the audiovisual equipment that we have right now?"

Answer: "I talked to my manager and asked him what he carried when we worked for his last company. I decided that I want to at least have as much for our company as he did for that one."

Probe: (C) "What was his annual expenditure over there?"

We have illustrated a variety of open and closed probes in this section. Without doubt, you can ask quite a few closed-ended probes in the time that it may take you to listen to the answer from one open probe. This is why so many people choose to use closed-ended probes. However, there are at least three compelling reasons to consider using the open-ended variety. First, open-ended probes allow the respondent to define the question from his or her own perspective, rather than using yours. You will learn what is important to the other person. Second, they allow the other person to volunteer information that you may not have thought to ask for. Third, because you are allowing the person to open up and talk, he or she may reveal some misunderstanding of crucial concepts and ideas. People may not demonstrate misunderstanding in a series of "yes" or "no" answers, but are more likely to do so with the longer answers that you receive with open-ended probes.

Pauses

Pauses are silent. Silence is very effective during fact-finding. Sometimes silence works well because it encourages the respondent to offer more information about a certain point. This is why you find many salespeople using pauses during attempts to close a sale.

We all feel the need to fill silence with words. It takes practice to use pauses effectively and to feel comfortable with the silence. The average amount of time between asking a question and providing an answer is three seconds—and that seems like an eternity. For an experiment have someone keep time and try to tell him or her when one minute of silence has passed. You will no doubt call time before the minute is up.

Restatements

A restatement is a repetition of what the respondent has just said in his or her own words, with no new ideas added. Restatements can function as follow-up questions to a topic introduced with a general lead. When you use restatements with an upward inflection, you actually invite the other person to follow up with an answer. In some cases, he or she may actually correct you, as a restatement invites the respondent to say more in a discreet fashion.

In all cases, you use the other person's exact words back. Examples of original statements and restatements include:

- "I'm concerned about whether this might get out to the media."

  "You're concerned about whether this might get out to the media."

- "I may not have enough money to hire someone to fill the position."

  "You may not have enough money to hire someone to fill the position."

- "Our regular customers seem satisfied with these services."

  "Your regular customers seem satisfied with these services."

- "I've had bad luck with employees with no experience."

  "You've had bad luck with employees with no experience."

Interpretations

The last, and perhaps riskiest, of all the communication tactics is an interpretation. Interpretations restate what the respondent said, but you add something new and/or change the information in some way.

Interpretations are useful for moving deeper into the subject that you brought up with a general lead and in linking several topics together. Like restatements, they are most often used with an upward inflection. Interpretations always leave room for the other person to correct the phrase, because you may have misstated his or her meaning. This opportunity for correction helps you keep your facts straight.

The risk you take when you use interpretations is that some people do not like another person putting words into their mouths. However, interpretations are useful in moving the conversation along, demonstrating your understanding of the information, and drawing relationships among seemingly unrelated factors.

Here are some examples of original lines and interpretations:

- "We hire contractors when we are under a time crunch."

  "So, you use contractors when you are under a time crunch; I assume that you have never considered hiring any of them full-time?"

- "I have recently remarried."

  "You have recently remarried, and you now feel the need to ensure that you are caring for your family properly?"

- "Saving money is not a priority to me."

  "Saving money is not a priority to you. Am I correct that you have several substantial policies to take care of you when you retire?"

- "I'm upset about the way my managers fail to follow up."

  "You're upset about the way that your managers fail to follow up, and I suppose that you would be very interested in a management tracking system that requires very little hands-on work?"

- "We don't offer our salespeople any incentives or commissions."

  "You don't offer your salespeople any incentives or commissions; does that mean that you do not participate in any discount buying programs on the corporate level?"

- "I hold a staff meeting every Monday morning."

  "So you hold a staff meeting every Monday morning. Can I assume that you cover all the issues that you need to thoroughly at that time?"

- "We get a lot of phone calls from Spanish-speaking customers."

  "You receive a lot of phone calls from Spanish-speaking customers. Does this mean that you want to take lessons to improve your communication skills in that language as soon as possible?"

- "I think we have the best people because our profits are up."

  "You think you've got the best people because your profits are up; I guess that means that you reward them really well for their performance?"

Methods for Gathering Information*

Now that you are clear about the skills and techniques you can use to gather information during a change initiative, the next step is to decide on the method that you will use to do so. In this section we will review three methods by which you can gather information and use the fact-finding skills and communication tactics we have previously discussed. The methods are self-completion questionnaires; direct interviews; and focus groups.

The strategies for using these methods were covered in the Analysis chapter. This section explains how to create the necessary tools.

Self-Completion Questionnaires

Questionnaires are an effective way to gain information from a large sample of a population. How you construct the questions is very important. Poorly

---

*The information in this section is taken from Lee & Owens (2000).

constructed questionnaires allow for wide interpretation by each person who completes one, and therefore they provide little valuable information.

Questionnaires are limited in that they only provide the information requested. This limitation can be exacerbated if a questionnaire is returned anonymously. In that case there is no way to contact respondents if their answers deviate greatly from the responses of the rest of the sample. It would be valuable to know what unique experiences caused them to respond the way they did. One way around this particular difficulty is to distribute "confidential" instead of anonymous questionnaires. Of course, those questionnaires that are intended to be anonymous should remain anonymous. Because this makes it impossible for you to follow up with your respondents, you should carefully consider your options before selecting anonymity.

If you send out questionnaires confidentially, you should develop a number code system that you can use to trace a specific questionnaire to a list of names to help retrieve potentially valuable information. Make sure, however, that you inform all respondents that you will strictly observe the confidentiality of their responses.

Once you construct the questions you want to ask, have them approved by upper management and Human Resources, obtaining their endorsement to proceed. There may be some information that you are not allowed to ask because of labor union agreements or governmental regulations. Be prepared to provide upper management and HR with a written plan that details how you will select participants, assure anonymity, administer the questionnaire, and analyze and report the information. You should base your questions on the objectives for the project created during the Design phase.

For example, if the objective is to determine the technology skills of a workforce, use a question such as "What technology skills do you possess?" Then provide a multiple-choice list with the last one being "Other."

A poorly constructed question on the same topic would be open-ended without the list of choices, because the responses you receive would be phrased in many different ways and would be difficult for you to categorize.

Direct Interviews

Direct interviews have four advantages:

1. They are a direct link to persons who have unique information about the problem you are investigating.

2. They are structured by the elements of schedule and planning, contain specific rules, and have a specific focus.

3. They allow for the collection of immediate follow-up information.

4. You can easily analyze the results.

Note: Although this section focuses on structured interviews, do not overlook valuable information that might come out in informal conversations with individuals. Anything you hear or read may be useful later. Just remember to indicate when and where you obtained the information. Take notes, organize your information, and remember to review it as you proceed with your assessment and analyses.

The interviewer should prepare for the interviews, maintain control during the interviews, and analyze the results. Preparation includes studying any available handbooks and dictionaries to learn the jargon of the people you will be interviewing. As with self-completion questionnaires, you should have your questions reviewed and approved by upper management and HR.

Interviews provide you with the opportunity to expand on the questions you ask in a questionnaire. For example, if your objective is to determine the technology skills of the interviewees, ask the same question you would for the self-completion questionnaire ("What technology skills do you possess?") but add the questions, "What is your level of experience?" and "How did you gain your experience?"

Interviews attempt to reach deeper levels of information than questionnaires typically and reasonably can. Allow enough time in your schedule to conduct interviews as a follow-up to the data analyses from survey responses. You may find the analysis raises as many questions as answers. You should develop interview questions at the same time as the questionnaires, but you may need to adjust your questions just before the interviews begin based on the results you receive from analyzing the questionnaires.

Selecting Interviewees. Once you receive approval on the interview questions, the next step is to choose the persons to be interviewed. Often supervisors in certain departments want to provide you with a list of hand-selected employees to interview. Discourage them from this because these employees might not represent a random sample of the department, unit, or organization you are investigating. You may end up with employees who are generally perceived positively by their supervisor. Request a list of all persons who are among the population to be interviewed. Randomly select names based on the total number of names on the list, divided by twice the number of interviewees desired for the sample. For example, a reasonable sample size is 10 percent (Lee & Owens, 2000). So if you have a list with one thousand names and wish to have a 10 percent sample (one hundred interviewees), you need to select two hundred names, every fifth name on the list, for a random sample. These calculations are

$$1000 \times .10 = 100 \text{ (desired sample)}$$
$$100 \times 2 = 200 \text{ (random sample size)}$$
$$1000 \div 200 = 5 \text{ (every fifth name)}$$

Contact all employees whose names appear on this derived list and attempt to enlist their cooperation for the interview.

If a supervisor insists on hand-selecting those persons who will be interviewed, explain the disadvantages to this type of selection process, but abide by his or her wishes. However, you should make note of the selection process in any report where you are summarizing findings, such as during Analysis.

You must make a confidentiality agreement available for each employee interviewed. This will assure them of the anonymity of their responses and make them more open to giving you the information.

When calling potential interviewees, you will need to explain the purpose of the interview and enlist their cooperation. During this contact, explain:

- The purpose of the interview;
- Their role in the interview;

- The confidential nature of the interview data;
- How the information collected in the interview will be used and who will receive the data; and
- The potential impact on the organization.

Call employees on the derived list until you have scheduled the desired number of persons to interview (in the example above, call until you have commitments from one hundred people).

Scheduling Interviews. Consider all the following factors when scheduling interviews:

1. Schedule a specific time and place for the interviews. Be sure to conduct the interviews in a neutral location.
2. Leave a thirty- to forty-five-minute break between interviews.
3. Avoid scheduling interviews immediately before lunch or late in the day.
4. Make appointments directly with the interviewee rather than leaving messages.
5. Do not schedule interviews during or as a part of lunch.
6. Be present when the interviewee arrives.

Starting Interviews. You should not begin an interview with questions. First, put the interviewee at ease by again explaining the purpose of the interview and answering his or her questions. Second, show the interviewee the confidentiality statement from management. Third, ask the interviewee whether he or she objects to having the session tape recorded.

Explain that tape recording helps capture all of the information exactly as the interviewee expresses it, and it eliminates the need to interpret notes later, possibly omitting important points. Very few persons will object to having the session tape recorded. However, if an employee does object, you will have to slow the pace of the interview to obtain the detailed information by taking notes.

Conducting Interviews. After establishing rapport with the interviewee, begin the interview. Here are some suggestions for making the interview successful:

1. Arrange the room comfortably for the interview. Sit opposite the person so that eye contact is possible, but avoid putting a desk or

table between yourself and the interviewee. A table or desk puts up a subtle barrier that might influence the interview results. Rather, put two chairs on either side of a low, small table that can hold the tape recorder. Be certain that the table has a pad or cover so that if the table is used to set drinks (offer the interviewee a beverage) or papers on, there will be little distracting noise.

2. Focus your attention on the interviewee, and do not allow your mind to wander. You might want to probe an interviewee further on a particular statement.

3. Sequence questions from general to specific. Ask for concrete examples about statements made, ask key questions in more than one way, and rephrase questions that the interviewee does not understand.

4. Ask for constructive criticism, but keep the criticism focused on the problem, not on specific people. Discourage long discourses on what appear to be private gripes. Use the next question on the questionnaire to ask for a specific example to refocus the interview.

5. Ask if the opinions expressed by the interviewee are held generally through the organization or whether they are his or hers alone. (Remember, though, that the interviewees' comments are based on their own perceptions and are not absolute.)

6. Admit an error if you make one.

7. Avoid disagreeing with the interviewee as well as expressing sarcasm, correcting, and contradicting. If you find yourself in a personality conflict or a power struggle, simply terminate the interview.

8. Don't bring the interview to a stop abruptly. Conclude by summarizing the points made by the interviewee and thank him or her for the time and the valuable information.

Remember, one-to-one interviews are expensive in terms of time and money. A well-structured interview will minimize the use of both resources while still gaining the maximum amount of information.

Interviewer Skills. Above all, when personally interviewing someone, be a good listener. Remember, you are present to learn. Do not monopolize the airtime.

Here are certain skills that good interviewers must exhibit:

Initiate Get the session going and keep it moving through statements that clarify, summarize, and move.

Regulate Pace the session through summarizing or, if necessary, pointing out time restrictions.

Inform Provide information that the interviewee or group might not know.

Note: We use "group" here because the interviewer needs these same skills when conducting group interviews or focus groups (discussed later).

Support Discourage the interviewee from attacking the viewpoints of the organization or other members of the group. Regularly remind each interviewee or group member that the purpose of the session is to get his or her point of view, not to critique the views of others.

Evaluate Provide a reality check by reflecting what has been stated back to the interviewee or group in summary form.

Focus Groups

If your organization's job descriptions and job prerequisite skills are not accurate, you can convene focus groups to develop both of these to accurately reflect the position and the job incumbent. A focus group consists of current job incumbents and their supervisors, convened separately or jointly to determine the requirements for the initiative.

Keep the following considerations in mind when selecting focus group members:

• Participants should be considered exemplary workers by their supervisors and peers.

• Members should be assigned rather than volunteer. This will help ensure a representative sample. Volunteers will sometimes have their own agenda that precipitates their desire to participate. Personal agendas, while they often generate a lot of debate, are counterproductive to the purpose of the session. If the volunteer is highly verbal, has a strong personality, and is very persuasive, he or she might actually dominate the session, which will skew the results of the focus group and not accurately represent the description of the job holder.

There are several techniques used for conducting focus groups, some of which require reaching consensus. A well-established technique is a rank-and-order (RAO) technique, which seems to foster discussion and information exchange. With a large numbers of issues to discuss, the first RAO activity might arrange the issues identified during an initial analysis around some logical categories. The purpose of the focus group would then be to prioritize the issues in order of relative importance across the entire group. Follow these steps in conducting an RAO:

1. Provide a list of issues to be considered by each focus group member.

2. Request that each member individually prioritize each issue in the list in order of importance from 1 to n (the number of issues in the list).

3. Chart the prioritized number of each of the issues on the list.

4. Sum the group's responses and divide by the number of responses.

5. Rewrite the list in the prioritized format, with numbers closer to 1 at the top, indicating that the group considered them more important.

Now that you've learned a number of techniques for gathering information, we will turn to the topic of disseminating that information.

14

Disseminating Information

THERE IS A STRONG RELATIONSHIP between individuals' receptivity toward change and the quality of communication about the initiative. While not everyone agrees with the maxim, "I can take good news or bad news, but no surprises," a proactive approach to communication throughout a change initiative pays large dividends.

In this chapter, we focus on ways to release information to others during a change initiative. We discuss some considerations for the all-important kickoff meeting for your change initiative. We also discuss some pitfalls to avoid when disseminating information in other meetings or through other written or oral means.

Kickoff

As we discussed in Chapter 6 on the Planning phase, a kickoff meeting for the change initiative is critical for your success, because it provides an opportunity for everyone affected to hear the same information at one time and for upper management, supervisors, and staff employees to exhibit support for the initiative. High quality and quantity of information is critical to the success of a change. At the kickoff, the focus is on the issue for the change. Each change steering committee member should explain his or her involvement and specify the function he or she will fulfill throughout the process. You should disseminate any information to employees that the company distributes to the media, not only in the early phases of the change initiative, but also throughout the initiative. No one likes to read a story about the organization in the newspaper and have friends or family call to ask you what you think about it, then receive a broadcast announcement about it through e-mail, voice mail, or a memo that afternoon. Employees should be the first to learn about company issues, not the media, and not the public.

The kickoff meeting is an excellent time for the change manager to "set the record straight" by debunking myths and dispelling rumors. The meeting provides the opportunity for all employees to ask questions, voice concerns, and reduce uncertainty. The meeting sets the tone for the entire change initiative that follows. Participants who speak during the kickoff meeting should be honest and thorough in their addresses to the group and enthusiastic about the change initiative. Excitement is contagious.

When one company we are familiar with acquired two smaller companies and integrated their products, brands, and services with its own, the rumors ran rampant about what would happen to existing jobs, functions, or services. Employees arrived at the kickoff meeting demoralized, confused, and disjointed. This meeting worked wonders to put a positive spin on the change. The CEO told employees that their jobs might change as a result of the acquisitions, but assured them that the company was committed to fair treatment and that everyone who had the potential to lose a job could interview for another within the company. The vice president for corporate communications announced the creation of a weekly newsletter and a special "hot line" for employees to call with questions. The vice president for information services announced new opportunities for employees to communicate their views online, as well as learn updated information on a daily basis. The kickoff gave the change process a terrific boost, and employees viewed it as a true new beginning, filled with unknown opportunities. Less than three years later, if you visited the company, you would never know that it had not always sponsored these brands and products.

To make a kickoff meeting successful, you should be sure that the highest possible ranking officers in the organization are in attendance, as well as the person or persons who are primarily in charge of carrying out the change effort. You want to make sure that these individuals are visible participants— not just attending, but speaking, mingling, and even lingering afterward to discuss and answer questions about the project.

Recognize that employees who attend this meeting do so under a cloud of uncertainty, suspicion, apprehension, and perhaps anger. In addition to being forthright and honest, the atmosphere should be upbeat and enthusiastic, in order to set the stage to champion the change that is announced. Consider playing rock-and-roll music, serving refreshments, distributing literature, and naming a theme for the meeting with costumed greeters at the door and others working their way through the crowd.

On a content level, the kickoff meeting should include:

- A clear statement about what the issue is and what change is going to accomplish with respect to corporate goals;

- How the issue creates problems, if unaddressed;

- A tentative timeline of events;

- The purpose and rationale behind a possible change, along with a sense of the decision-making process that may lead to a change;

- Key players and their responsibilities in the change effort;

- Statements of confidence in the employees, decision, and process; and

- Time for questions, answers, and comments.

You can cover these items in any order that you think is best, but we suggest starting with the big picture of what the company is feeling and why, then working down to specific details that are available. The success of your kickoff meeting largely depends on how well you instill a proper attitude toward the change initiative in the employees who attend. You have done your job if they leave the meeting confident and reassured, yet challenged and with their self-esteem intact. This meeting process should be a pattern for all other company meetings throughout the change initiative.

Routine Dissemination

Before and after the kickoff meeting, you should routinely disseminate information. This dissemination can take both oral and written forms. For example, you can post short memos and other releases in work areas, as well as on the company intranet. Consider establishing a special site on the intranet where employees can post questions, view responses, make comments, and provide reactions. Conduct routine meetings throughout the change process to keep the verbal information flowing. If the company has a regular newsletter, publish information about the change in every issue. If no company newsletter exists, you can start one to publish information about the initiative status. The final section of this chapter includes recommendations for writing releases and memos.

If your change initiative involves a significant technological shift, the chosen vendor of the system that the organization will implement should provide names of other companies engaged in similar, but non-competitive businesses. Representatives of these companies can be sources of testimonials for your change initiative when invited to your meetings. Inspiring and useful information, delivered by an established user of the new technology, can be invaluable. This is particularly true if the person explains what the situation was like before the change and then extols the virtues of the change.

If the innovation involves technology, have committee members visit other companies that use the system that your organization is about to adopt. Provide advanced training for committee members on the technology. These sources of information can become a part of the formal and informal communications that you perpetuate throughout the organization.

You may wish to provide an emphasis on some smaller aspect of the change process. A large international company whose base was in the Northeast chose to relocate to a suburb of Dallas, Texas. For six months inside its building prior to the move, employees could visit the "Dallas Room," which contained editions of the daily paper, area maps, real estate information, demographic data, school district information, social and cultural opportunities, Chamber of Commerce literature, and phones with free long distance to area codes within the Dallas area. Anyone who chose not to relocate to Dallas could not have claimed to do so because he or she did not know enough about the city.

Conducting Meetings

Importance of Meetings

Meetings are critical for committees during a change initiative, including the steering committee and other splinter or subgroups that form after the kickoff meeting. Committees keep each member informed about what is happening in the overall change initiative. They clarify roadblocks or barriers that the organization must overcome that impact the tasks that others perform. They build synergy within teams because they give members a chance to get to know each other's strengths, preferences, and tendencies and give a forum in which they may display them.

How to Conduct a "Bad" Meeting

We want to keep this topic short. After all, we all know how to conduct "bad" meetings because we have participated in so many of them. People fail to show up on time; they do not bring the right information (usually because they do not know what information they need); key people are called away at the last minute or are removed from a meeting in progress, therefore, no decisions can be made; the meetings are disorganized and get off track; the meetings are so long that committee members do not have time to implement the very tasks that they are assigned or responsible for during the proceedings; and the list goes on and on.

Regarding the change steering committee, the change manager schedules the meetings and is the de facto leader of those meetings, even though he or she may assign someone else to conduct the meeting. For example, the meeting may focus on an issue that another committee member has raised. The change manager will probably not be present for many subgroup meetings, so each meeting of this sort also needs to have an identified leader. Most likely, the leader for those meetings is also the person assigned the responsibility for the task on the Project Management Tool. So it is important that everyone know how to conduct a "good" meeting—a meeting where things get done in a minimum of time.

Components of a "Good" Meeting

We use the terms "bad" and "good" even though they are very subjective—we may not know what it means, but we know what it is when we see it! Now we are going to provide some objectivity to these terms.

Good meetings are pretty much the opposite of a bad meeting. A good meeting has the following characteristics:

- Participants receive requests for agenda items and receive agendas at least a day in advance of the meeting.

- Everyone arrives with a common understanding of the purpose and goals of the meeting.

- Everyone knows how long the meeting will last so they can plan the rest of the day.

- Participants are clear about the way that the meeting will be conducted.

- Each agenda item has a time limit for presentation and discussion, and the leader for the meeting enforces these limits.

- People feel comfortable to communicate, provide inputs, and disagree.

- Everyone participates—many are even assigned roles that they assume during the meeting. However, only people who need to attend the meeting are invited. Others are notified in case they want to sit in.

- Meetings are critiqued and everyone feels comfortable stating it if they feel meetings are going poorly. A "parliamentarian" might be assigned to keep the meeting on track and maintain adherence to the agenda.
- Participants receive the minutes of meeting discussions, decisions, and action items taken by the day following the meeting.
- Meetings begin and end on time. They can run over only with the agreement of the entire group.

The change manager should review the rules for subsequent meetings at the first change steering committee meeting, as well as model the way he or she expects others to conduct meetings as a part of their responsibility.

Change steering committee meetings or subgroup committee meetings should:

- Inform committee members of the progress on their tasks or tasks from related subgroups;
- Involve a discussion of any barriers or obstacles that have arisen for the work team (which will probably slow the progress of the total initiative) that need to be overcome to continue;
- Decide how to eliminate the barrier or obstacle; and
- Assign action items for those who must investigate issues, report back, or be responsible for addressing issues and solving problems.

Leaders of work group meetings should conduct these meetings in the same way. Meetings between two people (for example, change manager and committee member, committee leader and committee member, team leader and team leader) should also adhere to these guidelines, with the person who calls the meeting responsible for undertaking the leadership role. The topics and agendas for informal meetings or meetings between two people can be sent in an e-mail or explained over the phone.

Exhibit 14.1 contains an example of an agenda for a meeting. Exhibit 14.2 is a narrative agenda. Note that each team leader should be contacted ahead of time and asked for his or her agenda items and the approximate amount of time needed to cover those items.

Exhibit 14.1. Sample Agenda for Change Steering Committee.

Change Steering Committee

Date: _____   Time: _____

Item	Person Responsible	Outcome Needed	Time
Review of Agenda and Purpose of the Meeting	Bill [Change Manager]	• Understand items • Add last-minute issues since agenda was distributed	2 minutes
Update from Each Work Group	Doris Ed Mike Kay [Each Team Lead]	• Understanding of progress on tasks, activities, action items since last meeting	Doris: 5 minutes Ed: 10 minutes Mike: 3 minutes Kay: 7 minutes Total: 25 minutes
Obstacles and Barriers	Bill Kay	• Bill: Decision on how to proceed to remove the obstacle of . . . • Kay: Decision on how to proceed to remove the obstacle of . . . [Note: Doris, Ed, Mike do not have agenda items.]	Bill: 10 minutes Kay: 10 minutes
Added Agenda Items	Whoever Added the Item	• Whatever is needed (that is, discussion, decision, assistance)	Whatever time is requested when item is added
Assign Action Items	Bill	• Decision on information that needs to be presented at next meeting	5 minutes
Set Date and Time for Next Meeting	Bill	• Regular meeting: 10:00 a.m. Friday, March 20 • Kay's initiative team: 1:00 p.m. Monday, March 16 • Doris' initiative team: 9:30 a.m. Tuesday, March 17 • Ed's initiative team: 3:00 p.m. Tuesday, March 17 • Mike's initiative team: 8:00 a.m. Thursday, March 19	30 seconds

Exhibit 14.2. Sample Narrative Agenda.

Review of Agenda

Bill will:
- Open the meeting
- Review the purpose
- Review the agenda
- Clarify any questions from committee members
- Ask if there are any corrections to the minutes from the last meeting [previously distributed]

Update from Each Work Group

Each team leader or representative will explain the progress his or her team has made since the last meeting and explain progress on any action items from the last or past meetings.

Obstacles

Each team lead or representative will explain the obstacle(s) that his or her team has encountered since the last meeting and either ask for input on how to proceed or explain to the committee the action he or she took to remove or overcome the obstacle.

Added Agenda Items

These items are those that have arisen since the agenda was distributed, but which need discussion or resolution before the next regular meeting.

Action Items

Through these discussions, participants should be clear what action items each committee member needs to take. However, Bill should go over each of them, ensuring an assignment for every item and that the person assigned understands what type of action is needed and the time frame for a response.

Dates and Times for Next Meetings

Bill will review the dates and times for this week's regularly scheduled meetings and any special meetings that have been called.

Releases and Memos

We recommend that a specialist in corporate communications who has expertise in writing releases and memos for the media, company newsletters, or the corporate intranet participate on the change steering committee. Such a person may not be available, in which case other committee members may need to perform this function.

Here are some guidelines to follow in order to maximize your potential for success in communicating written information about your change initiative:

- The best written pieces are informative, rather than persuasive. Be sure to include details such as who, what, where, when, and why. Remember to be short and concise.

- Write a headline so that an editor will know the most important element in your copy.

- Include a release date to let an editor know when you want the information disseminated.

- Include your own contact information, including your name, address, phone, fax, and e-mail address, so that the editor can reach you if he or she has questions about your piece.

- Put the most important information first, then develop additional details.

- Double-space the copy so that the editor has room to make changes.

- Put "END" at the conclusion of the copy.

- Double-check everything: facts, dates, spelling, and grammar.

WE HOPE YOU HAVE REACHED THESE FINAL PAGES of our book in a state of mind about change that is energetic, motivated, and anticipatory about enacting an initiative. We also hope that the tools that we have provided for you in the various chapters and on the CD-ROM have assisted you in making some important decisions with confidence along the way. Remember that you can use the "cube" as an index to help you locate specific roles and responsibilities for each stakeholder in the process.

As you begin work on organizing your change initiative, we want to make a few final reflections about what you have read.

Change As a Constant

Many organization development practitioners and consultants have popularized the notion that "change is constant," "change is inevitable," and "the only thing you can count on is that things will change." We have not taken issue with these premises. You are well aware that change is all around you in every aspect of your personal and professional life. We also believe that change is a healthy feature of organization life and, therefore, you should take advantage of the potential that change brings you for producing gains in productivity, profitability, and other desirable results.

If we could sum up what we have tried to say about the inevitability of change in this book, it is simply that, if change is inevitable, then drive it—don't experience it. Change will happen. You cannot stop it. Using an aircraft analogy, you have two choices. You can choose to be either a passenger or a pilot.

In a passenger role, you experience change only as you become aware of it. You are passive. You are reactive. You follow. We think that any gains that may accrue to a "passenger" as a result of the change are minimized or compromised, perhaps even coincidental, rather than optimal.

In a pilot role, you chart and then fly a course of action. You make decisions about where you go, how you get there, and when to get there. You are active. In fact, you are actually proactive. You lead. The benefits that you and your organization realize from the change are varied and go beyond what you or anyone else may even anticipate.

You will approach change in the driver's seat rather than in the passenger's seat if you execute the various tasks we describe in this book and complete the numerous tools along the way. Further, you allow many participants across the entire organization to take a driver's role as well, which maximizes their involvement, commitment, and contribution.

The Time Factor

We cannot argue with you if, on reaching these final pages, you are thinking: "This was good, but we just do not have the time to do all these steps and get this many people involved. We have to move quickly." The process of organizing change in the manner we have described in this book does take some time to execute. You have important decisions to make about people, paths, and priorities. Rushing through any point of the process can cause you to obtain results from a change initiative that are less than optimal, or even less than desirable.

We readily admit that this process is time-consuming. You could save time by just announcing a change initiative, whether that is a new policy, procedure, method, rule, product, or service, and then allowing people to execute their roles and responsibilities on a trial-and-error basis. Our response to this dilemma is actually quite dated: "Do you want to pay me now, or pay me later?"

Our premise is that by organizing change in the way that we have laid out for you here, you will save more time, save more money, avoid potentially embarrassing situations, and work in a higher quality manner than you will if you have to clean up a mess later. A poorly executed change initiative will require you to spend more time, more money, and more effort repairing damaged internal and external relationships than you would ever have spent had you taken the time to do it right in the first place.

We do not suggest that our approach is what you might label a "cookie-cutter" variety. You have plenty of options available by which you can tailor and customize the various components of this process to the needs and preferences of your own organization. However, we do think that discipline is important, especially the first time that you use a process such as this. By "discipline" we mean that you must budget the time to execute each step of the process in the proper manner and that you will finish with the feeling that you have invested the proper amount of energy, attention, and resources.

Organizing change is all about preparing and executing. Doing it right takes time and money. Short-cutting it wastes time and money. Pay yourself dividends by making a conscious decision to invest the proper resources to make the process successful.

Overcoming Resistance

Early in the book, we voiced our view that people dislike change "done poorly" rather than simply change itself. Our premise has been that, when people are informed and involved in a well-executed and organized change initiative, their receptivity to the change is positive, not negative.

We cannot change human nature. Most people have an adverse reaction to altering a system or process that they are used to, especially one that has worked well for them. Everyone will not share the same levels of enthusiasm about initiating a change as those who originally devise the change plan.

The process you have experienced in this book allows for a variety of participants in the change initiative to not only provide a rationale for making the change, but also for those affected to work in a check-and-balance system to test the assumptions and viability of a proposal. We think, given these widespread opportunities for voice, involvement, and participation, that participants who continually cry that they do not "like" the change will quickly lose sympathy and credibility with their peers. As more and more people see their interests represented, their ideas considered and implemented, and their feelings considered, the organization can more easily win over those who doubt or resist.

When you consider the stark alternative of the organization simply announcing, "This is the way it is going to be," our approach is a better and systematic way to overcome objections by involving people throughout the process. We do not believe it is a waste of time for stakeholders to anticipate objections and prepare answers to them. We do believe it is ludicrous for stakeholders to think that simply providing answers will satisfy those affected by change in an organization. People want to be involved in decisions that affect how they work, and providing a system-wide method for involving them is the best way to overcome resistance.

Final Thought

You have likely read about the "scarcity" versus the "abundance" mentality. Simply put, advocates of the abundance mentality in organizations believe that abilities are widespread, that there are plenty of opportunities for many people to partake of, and that gains by one person or division do not come at the expense of others. An abundance mentality is not a zero-sum game that operates from a finite set of resources.

We believe that our approach represents the best of the abundance mentality. Throughout these chapters, we have encouraged you and provided you methods to obtain widespread participation and input from a variety of sources throughout an organization that handles a change initiative. Contrast this approach with one that says that only a few at the top of an organization know what is right or good for everyone else.

Human beings at all levels of an organization are wonderful sources of knowledge, experiences, and ideas. There are plenty of people with plenty of ways to contribute. A successful change initiative is one that takes advantage of this resource by encouraging participation and harnessing enthusiasm. This method is inclusive, systematic, and systemic. For those who follow our approach, great gains in productivity await you. Why would you want to proceed in any other way?

We wish you all the very best in your change initiative.

REFERENCES

Benne, K., & Sheats, P. (1948). Functional roles of group members. *The Journal of Social Issues, 4*(2), 41–49.

Bridges, W. (1991). *Managing transitions: Making the most of change.* Cambridge, MA: Perseus.

Brynjolfsson, E., Hitt, L., & Yang, S. (2002). *Intangible assets: How the interaction of computers and organizational structure affects stock market valuations.* Unpublished study.

Burns, R. B. (1993). *Managing people in changing times: Coping with the human impact of organizational change.* St Leonards, New South Wales: Allen & Unwin.

Carey, L., & Dick, W. (1990). *The systematic design of instruction* (3rd ed.). Glenview, IL: Scott, Foresman.

Collins, J. (2001). *Good to great: Why some companies make the leap . . . and others don't.* New York: HarperCollins.

Gagne, R., Briggs, L., & Wager, W. (1988). *Principles of instructional design* (3rd ed.). New York: Holt, Rinehart & Winston.

Galinksy, E., Kim, S., & Bond, J. T. (2001). *Feeling overworked: When work becomes too much.* New York: Families and Work Institute.

Hamel, G. (2000). *Leading the revolution.* Boston, MA: Harvard Business School Press.

Jeffreys, J. (1995). *Coping with workplace change: Dealing with loss and grief.* Menlo Park, CA: Crisp.

Kotter, J. P. (1996). *Leading change.* Boston, MA: Harvard Business School Press.

Kotter, J. P., & Cohen, D. S. (2002). *The heart of change.* Boston, MA: Harvard Business School Press.

Lee, W., & Owens, D. (2000). *Multimedia-based instructional design: Computer-based training, web-based training, distance broadcast training.* San Francisco, CA: Jossey-Bass/Pfeiffer.

Lee, W., & Roadman, K. (1991). Linking needs assessment to performance based evaluation. *Performance & Instruction, 30*(6), 4–6.

Litchfield, L., & Pitt-Catsouphes, M. (1999). *Culture and work/life balance: Findings from the* Business Week *study.* Chestnut Hill, MA: Boston College Center for Work and Family.

Lucia, A., & Lepsinger, R. (1999). *The art and science of competency models: Pinpointing critical success factors in organizations.* San Francisco, CA: Jossey-Bass/Pfeiffer.

McGarvey, R. (2002). Getting up from down. *American Way, 6*(1), 66–69.

Noer, D. M. (1995). *Healing the wounds: Overcoming the trauma of layoffs and revitalizing downsized organizations.* San Francisco, CA: Jossey-Bass.

Osborn, A. F. (1993). *Applied imagination.* Hadley, MA: Creative Education Foundation.

Pande, P., Neuman, R., & Cavanaugh, R. (2000). *The six sigma way: How GE, Motorola, and other top companies are honing their performance.* New York: McGraw-Hill.

Petty Productions. (1991). *The Deming of America* [video]. Cincinnati, OH: Author.

Phillips, J., & Stone, R. (2002). *How to measure training results.* New York: McGraw-Hill.

Pritchett, P., & Pound, R. (1992). *Business as unusual: The handbook for managing and supervising organizational change.* Dallas, TX: Pritchett Publishing.

Pritchett, P., & Pound, R. (1993). *A survival guide to the stress of organizational change.* Dallas, TX: Pritchett Publishing.

The Quality Improvement Company. (1994). *Continuous improvement workshop.* Cupertino, CA: Author.

Rogers, E. M. (1983). *Diffusion of innovation.* New York: The Free Press.

Schrock, S., Coscarelli, W., & Eyres, P. (2000). *Criterion-referenced test development.* Gaithersburg, MD: ISPI Publications.

Seels, B., & Glasgow, Z. (1990). *Exercises in instructional design.* Columbus, OH: Merrill.

Senge, P. (1990). *The fifth discipline: The art and practice of the learning organization.* New York: Doubleday.

Smith, H. (2001). *Juggling work and family.* Boston, MA: Public Broadcasting System.

Smith, R. (1997). *The seven levels of change: Create, innovate and motivate with the secrets of the world's largest companies.* Arlington, TX: Summit Publishing Group.

Useem, M. (2001). *Leading up: How to lead your boss so you both win.* New York: Crown.

Watkins, J., & Mohr, B. (2001). *Appreciative inquiry.* San Francisco, CA: Jossey-Bass/Pfeiffer.

ABOUT THE AUTHORS

William W. Lee, Ph.D., is probably better know to everyone by his nickname "Bill." He is the principal consultant for his own independently owned business, ETC Educational Technologies Consulting, and a senior consultant for Training Consulting Softek. He has worked for American Airlines, EDS, Ferranti Defense Systems, Ford Motor Training, and the Country of Singapore. His fields of expertise are in e-learning, organizational change, instructional design, and evaluation. He has conducted numerous performance improvement and return-on-investment studies for the companies he has worked for, developed evaluation strategies for those companies, and instituted their e-learning strategies. He provided American Airlines with its Corporate University Model and was one of four managers of the institute for three years. He has been the director of multimedia sales and marketing. Bill teaches on the faculty of two universities, the University of Oklahoma and the University of Texas at Dallas, in their professional development programs, teaching workshops in media analysis, web design, and human performance improvement.

Bill is the author of two books on the design, development, and implementation of e-learning. In this book he uses his background in the field of instructional design to apply those concepts to corporate issues with much broader scope than training. That scope increases to examining non-training issues that impact a solution and expanding to enterprise-wide solutions or departmental solutions. Bill is an internationally known speaker and author. He works extensively with international ASTD, as well as with his local chapter in Dallas, Texas. His latest book on multimedia instructional design, published by Jossey-Bass/Pfeiffer, has been translated into Japanese, Chinese, and Korean.

Bill received his M.Ed. and Ph.D. from Penn State University and his undergraduate degree from Clarion University of Pennsylvania.

Karl J. Krayer received his Ph.D. from the University of Oklahoma, specializing in organizational communication. He is the president of Creative Communication Network, a full-service company offering speeches and presentations, training, custom consulting, and meeting facilitation for individuals, groups, and organizations.

Karl is a nationally renowned speaker, author, and consultant who works with corporations and associations that want to assess and improve competency, teamwork, and communication. He also provides informative, dynamic, and entertaining presentations and workshops for small businesses that want to increase productivity and profitability. Karl served on the faculties of Auburn and Texas Christian Universities before beginning a ten-year stint with Dr Pepper/Seven Up, Inc., as a training manager. He is a past president of the Dallas chapter of the American Society for Training and Development and was named its "Professional of the Year" in 1990. He is an active member of the National Speakers Association and the DFW Organization Development Network. During 2001–2002, he served the National Speakers Association of North Texas as president. Karl's training and organization development interventions at Dr Pepper/Seven Up yielded significant results for the corporation in productivity, profitability, and return on investment.

His internal consulting efforts were instrumental in leading work reorganization and process improvement changes for the corporation's marketing and marketing services divisions. Karl now serves as an adjunct faculty member in the University of Dallas Graduate School of Management, teaching courses in human behavior in organizations. Karl has presented addresses to conferences of more than seventy-five professional and academic associations and has written more than thirty articles in refereed trade, industrial, and academic publications. In 1999, he published a chapter in a book in the national ASTD "In-Action" Series entitled *Effective Leadership Programs;* in 2001, he published a chapter in an anthology entitled *The Leadership Path;* and in 2002, he published chapters in *The Communication Path* and *Back to Basics.* His specialties include competency assessment, management and leadership development, training and organization development, communication, and interpersonal relationships. Karl's featured workshop, Manager-as-Trainer, is designed to provide managers who are not professional trainers with the techniques and tools to develop their direct reports in order to improve competency and achieve organizational outcomes.

INDEX

A

Adams, F., 73–75

Agendas, meeting, 64

Albertson, J., 74–76

Allen, M., 81

American Society for Training and Development, 115

Analysis phase: analysis report in, 122, 124; case studies of, 124–134; change manager's duties in, 108–109; critical incident analysis in, 111, 120–121; environmental analysis for, 111, 117–118; extant data analysis in, 111, 114–116; human resources' duties in, 109, 110; inputs in, 107; issue analysis in, 111, 118–119; management information services' duties in, 109, 110; outputs of, 108; overview of, 107; problems and solutions in, 135; purpose of, 25; skill gap analysis in, 111–114; staff's duties in, 109, 110; supervisor's duties in, 108, 109; technology analysis in, 111, 121–122, 123–124; training/performance analyst's duties in, 109–110; types of analyses in, 111; upper management's duties in, 108, 109

Anderson, T., 74

Appreciative Inquiry, 120

Assessment phase: case studies in, 96–103; change manager's duties in, 91, 92; human resources' duties in, 91, 93; inputs in, 89; management information services' duties in, 91, 93; methodology in, 95–96; outputs in, 90; overview of, 89; problems and solutions in, 103–105; purpose of, 25; staff's duties in, 91, 93; supervisor's duties in, 90, 91–92; training/performance analyst's duties in, 91, 92–93; upper management's duties in, 90, 91

Assessment, project, 141, 142–145

Attitudes, employee, 37, 38, 226–227

Attrition plans, 163

B

Barry, S., 75

Beene, K., 46–47

Behavioral interviewing, 41, 43, 44

Bekins, H., 81

Benchmarking. *See* Extant data analysis

Bennett, H., 81

Blumroth case study, 73–76, 96–99, 124–130, 148–152, 164–166, 175–176, 195–196

Bond, J. T., 38

Bridges, W., 16

Burn out, 7

Burns, R. B., 6

C

Case studies: in assessment phase, 96–103; Blumroth, 73–76, 124–130, 148–152, 164–166, 175–176, 195–196; in design phase, 148–156; in development phase, 164–168; evaluation phase, 195–198; Northcutt Health Solutions, 76–85, 99–103, 130–134, 152–156, 166–168, 176–178, 197–198; in planning phase, 73–85; SAP company, 71–76, 98–99, 149–152, 165–166, 175–176, 195–196

CD-ROM, 12, 255–256

Change: as constant, 235–236; imposed by management, 5; levels of, 7–9; need for quick reaction to, 16; organizing versus reacting to, 8; people's dislike for, 5, 237–238; recovery from, 18–19

Change agents. *See* Stakeholders

Change initiatives: benefits of organization in, 1–2; characteristics of successful, 1; definition of, 21; dependent nature of, 17; interaction effects of, 6–7; performance analysis of, 184; required time for, 18, 236–237

Change managers: accessibility of, 31–32; analysis phase duties of, 108–109; assessment phase duties of, 91, 92; definition of, 24; design phase duties of, 138, 139; development phase duties of, 160, 161–163; evaluation phase duties of, 182, 183; external consultants as, 32; implementation phase duties of, 172, 173; as meeting leader, 230; overview of duties of, 31–33; planning phase duties of, 61, 63–64; selection of, 32; and steering committee interaction, 45, 46

Change model, 9, 22–26, 26

Change process, 21, 25, 36. *See also specific phases of change process*

Change steering committee: analyzing interactions of, 49–56; completion of Project Management Tool by, 66–71; definition of, 24; interaction styles of, 46–49; members of, 30–31; recognition of, 33–34; roles of group members in, 46–49; selection of members in, 39–44; as team, 64

Churchill, J., 81

Cisterian, H., 74

Closed probes, 11–212, 213–214

Coaching, 92

Collins, J., 18

Communication: characteristics of, 205; definition of, 21, 145; to gather information, 210–217; of ideas, 35; levels of, 204–205; overview of, 26, 203; quality and quantity of information in, 203–204; of steering committee members, 46–56

Communication specialist, 25, 35

Competition, 10

Computer systems, 35–36

Confidentiality, 218, 220

Cooperation, 10, 64

Copying level of change, 7

Corporate communication specialist, 35

Corporate Leadership Council, 115

Corporate University Exchange, 115

Correlations, 192

Coscarelli, W., 190

Cost/benefit ratio, 108, 187–190

Counseling, 37

Critical incident analysis, 111, 120–121

Criticism, 222

Culture, diversity of, 76

Culture, organizational, 16–17, 144

Curtis, M., 81

Cutting level of change, 7

D

Data analysis, 186–187

Davis, C., 79–85

Davis, L., 83–84, 99

Davis, S., 81

The Deming of America (Deming), 30

Deming, W. E., 30

Design phase: case studies of, 148–156; change manager's duties in, 138, 139; design report in, 148; human resources' duties in, 138, 140; inputs in, 137; instructional analysis in, 141, 142; management information services' duties in, 138, 140–141; outputs in, 137; overview of, 137; problems and solutions in, 157; purpose of, 25; staff's duties in, 138, 140; supervisor's duties in, 138, 139; training/performance analyst's duties in, 138, 139–140; upper management's duties in, 138–139

Disseminating information. *See* Information dissemination

Development phase: case studies of, 164–168; change manager's duties in, 160, 161–163; human resources' duties in, 160, 163–164; inputs in, 159; management information services' duties in, 160, 164; outputs in, 159; overview of, 159; problems and solutions in, 168–169; purpose of, 25; staff's duties in, 160, 164; supervisor's duties in, 160, 161; training/performance analyst's duties in, 160, 163; upper management's duties in, 160

Different level of change, 7

Difficulty index, 191

Direct interviews, 219–223

Diversity, 76

Dot-com's, 16

Downsizing: attrition plan for, 163; best methods of, 37; counseling prior to, 37; disadvantages of, 6–7; employees' attitudes during, 37, 38; resignations during, 163

Duncan, B., 74

E

Effectiveness level of change, 7

Efficiency level of change, 7

Elements, 118, 120

Employees: effects of downsizing on, 7; and growth of business organization, 16; involvement of, 30; in merged business organizations, 16–17; organized exchanges for, 140; reason for resistance in, 22; rumors among, 226–227; support for, 35, 37; view of external consultant, 32; and work-life balance, 38. *See also* Staff; Teams

Environmental analysis, 111, 117–118

Evaluation phase: change agents' duties in, 182–186; data analysis in, 186–187; inputs in, 181; outputs in, 182; overview of, 181; problems and solutions in, 199–200; purpose of, 25

Evaluation Plan, 148, 192–194

Executive summary, 193

Expectations, 145

Extant data analysis, 111, 114–116

External consultants, 32–33

Eyres, P., 190

F

Fact-finding, 205–210

Farve, M., 80

The Fifth Discipline (Senge), 17

Financial analyst, 25, 35

Focus groups, 223–224

Franklin, B., 78–83

Franklin, L., 75

Frequency counts, 190–191

Functional operations manager, 183

G

Galinksy, E., 38

Gathering information. *See* Information gathering

General leads, 210–211

Good to Great (Collins), 18

H

Hamel, G., 6

Hanratty, L., 80

Hardage, E., 76

Hardesty, T., 80

Harold, B., 75

The Heart of Change (Kotter), 6

Human resources: analysis phase duties of, 109, 110; assessment phase duties of, 91, 93; definition of, 24; design phase duties of, 138, 140; development phase duties of, 160, 163–164; evaluation phase duties of, 182, 185; implementation phase duties of, 172, 173–174; overview of duties of, 37–38; planning phase duties of, 61, 64–65

I

Idea generation, 9–10, 35

Implementation phase: case studies of, 175–178; change manager's duties in, 173; human resources' duties in, 172, 173–174; inputs in, 171; management information services' duties in, 172, 174; outputs in, 172; overview of, 171; problems and solutions in, 178–179; purpose of, 25; recognition for, 34; staff's duties in, 172, 174; supervisor's duties in, 172, 173; support of employees during, 35; training/performance analyst's duties in, 172, 173; upper management's duties in, 172

Impossible level of change, 7

Improving level of change, 7

Incentives, 145

Inclusive change approach, 1, 8, 11

Individual rating method, 41, 42, 43

Individual roles, 47

Information dissemination: definition of, 26; kickoff meeting for, 226–228; memos for, 234; overview of, 225; releases for, 234; routine methods of, 228–229

Information exchange, 203–205

Information gathering: communication for, 210–216; definition of, 26; during evaluation phase, 186; during extant data analysis, 115–116; fact-finding for, 205–210; methods for, 217–224

Instruction, in change process, 36

Instructional analysis, 141, 142

Interaction. *See* Communication

Internet, 16, 115

Interpretations, 216–217

Interview instruments, 190

Interviewee selection, 220–221

Interviewing method: of committee selection, 41, 43, 44; for information gathering, 219–223

Interviews, direct, 219–223

Intranet, 228

Issue analysis, 111, 118–119

Issues, 118, 120, 142, 144

Item analysis, 191

J

Jeffreys, J., 6

Job descriptions, 112

K

Kendall, J., 75

Kickoff meeting, 29–30, 36, 62, 226–228

Kim, S., 38

Knowledge, skills, and attitudes (KSA), 112, 145

Kotter, J. P., 6

Krayer, K. J., 4–5, 41

L

Layoffs. *See* Downsizing

Leading Change (Kotter), 6

Leading the Revolution (Hamel), 6

Leading Up (Useem), 6

Lee, W., 3–5, 41, 95, 121, 142, 145, 188, 190, 220

Lepsinger, R., 95

Listening, 208

Litchfield, L., 38

Lucia, A., 95

M

Maintenance roles, 46

Management. *See* Upper management

Management information services: analysis phase duties of, 109, 110; assessment phase duties of, 91, 93; definition of, 24; design phase duties of, 138, 140–141; development phase duties of, 160, 164; evaluation phase duties of, 182, 186; implementation phase duties of, 172, 174; overview of duties of, 35–36; planning phase duties of, 61, 65

Matrix organization, 77–78

McGarvey, R., 7

Measurement instruments, 190–192. *See also specific instruments*

Meetings: agendas for, 64, 230, 231–233; characteristics of bad, 229–230; components of good, 230–231; importance of, 229

Memos, 234

Merged business organization, 16–17

Mirror questions, 210

Mission statement, 94, 147

Mohr, B., 120

N

Narrative agenda, 231, 233

Nelson, H., 75

Net profit, 188

Net program benefits, 188

Newsletters, 228

Noer, D. M., 6

Northcutt Health Solutions, 76–85, 99–103, 130–134, 152–156, 166–168, 176–178, 197–198

O

Objectives, 145–148, 218

Observation: during environmental analysis, 117; for fact-finding, 207–208, 208; of steering committee interaction, 49–51

Online searches, 115

Open probes, 211, 213–214

Organization, benefits of, 1–2

Organization, business: culture after merger of, 16–17; dependent nature of, 17; growth of complexity in, 15–17; life expectancy of, 17

Organization development analyst, 25

Organizational Development Network, 115

Organizational structure, 145

Owens, D., 95, 121, 142, 145, 188, 190, 220

P

Pauses, 215

Performance improvement interventions, 36

Performance issues, 142

Petty Productions, 30

Pilot test, 169, 171, 174

Pitt-Catsouphes, M., 38

Planning phase: change manager's duties in, 61, 63–64; human resources' duties in, 61, 64–65; input of, 60; management information services' duties in, 61, 65; Northcutt Health Solutions case study in, 76–85; output of, 60; overview of, 59–60; problems and solutions in, 85–87; purpose of, 25; SAP company's case study, 71–76; staff's duties in, 61, 65; supervisor's duties in, 61, 62–63; training/performance analyst's duties in, 61, 64; upper management's duties in, 60–62

Position description, 112

Position title, 112

Pound, R., 6

Pritchett, P., 6

Probes, 211–215

Procedures, 145

Process. *See* Change process

Processes, 145

Productivity, 7, 11, 184

Proficiency measures, 112

Profit, 188

Project, 118

Project assessment, 141, 142–145

Project Management Tool, 65, 66–71

Project Plan, 161–163

Q

Qualitative measures, 190

Questionnaires, 41–44, 190, 217–218

Questions: construction of, 218; in fact-finding, 208, 209; general leads as, 210–211; probing, 211–215

R

Random sample, 220

Rank-and-order technique, 224

Rating scales. *See specific rating scales*

Recognition, 33–34

Reflective questions, 210

Releases, 234

Resignations, 163

Resistance to change, 5, 22, 237–238

Restatements, 210, 215

Retention, 144

Return on investment analysis, 187–190

Richardson, B., 75

Rogers, E. M., 41

Rumors, 226–227

S

SAP company, 71–76, 98–99, 149–152, 165–166, 175–176, 195–196

Scheduling interviews, 221

Schrock, S., 190

Self-completion questionnaires, 217–218

Senge, P., 17

Severance packages, 163, 174

Sheats, P., 46–47

Silence, 215

Skill gap analysis, 111–114

Skills, 112, 145

Smith, H., 38

Smith, R., 7

Society for Human Resource Management, 115

Staff: analysis phase duties of, 109, 110; assessment phase duties of, 91, 93; definition of, 24; design phase duties of, 138, 140; development phase duties of, 160, 164; evaluation phase duties of, 182, 185–186; implementation phase duties of, 172, 174; overview of duties of, 35; planning phase duties of, 61, 65. *See also* Employees; Teams

Stakeholders: definition of, 21; duties of, 30–38; overview of, 24–25, 29–30

Statistician, 35, 186

Steering committee. *See* Change steering committee

Sub-elements, 118

Sunk costs, 190

Supervisors: analysis phase duties of, 108, 109; assessment phase duties of, 90–92; definition of, 24; design phase duties of, 138, 139; development phase duties of, 160, 161; evaluation phase duties of, 182, 183; implementation phase duties of, 172, 173; overview of duties of, 34–35; planning phase duties of, 61, 62–63

Surveys, 41–44, 190

Systematic change approach, 8

Systemic change approach, 1, 8, 9

Systemic issues, 142

T

Task roles, 46

Teams, 9–10, 64. *See also* Employees

Teamwork, 10, 64

Technology analysis, 111, 121–122, 123–124

Technology systems, 35–36, 228–229

Tests of significance, 192

Tools, 145

Training, definition of, 145

Training issues, 144

Training/Performance analysts: analysis phase duties of, 109–110; assessment phase duties of, 91, 92–93; definition of, 24; design phase duties of, 138, 139–140; development phase duties of, 160, 163; evaluation phase duties of, 182, 184–185; implementation phase duties of, 172, 173; overview of duties of, 36; planning phase duties of, 61, 64

Turvein, L., 81

U

Upper management: analysis phase duties of, 108, 109; assessment phase duties of, 90, 91; definition of, 24; design phase duties of, 138–139; development phase duties of, 160; effects of change imposed by, 5; evaluation phase duties of, 182, 183; implementation phase duties of, 172; overview of duties of, 33–34; planning phase duties of, 60–62; selection of change manager by, 32

Useem, M., 6

V

Verbal communication, 205

W

Watkins, J., 120

Welch, J., 79

Work environment, 145

Work-life balance, 38

NOTE TO READER:

Printed in the United States
By Bookmasters